Hidden Investment
Treasures

Hidden Investment Treasures

How to Find Great Stock Investments as the Investment World Goes Passive

Daniel Gladiš

WILEY

Library of Congress Cataloging-in-Publication Data is Available:

ISBN 9781394344802 (Cloth)
ISBN 9781394344819 (ePub)
ISBN 9781394344826 (ePDF)

Cover Design: Wiley
Author Photo: Courtesy of the Author
Printed and bound by CPI Group (UK) Ltd, Croydon, CR0 4YY

C9781394344802_140126

*Dedicated to Pavel's memory.
Fate did not afford him time to enjoy
the compound interest on his investments.*

Contents

Foreword

By John Mihaljevic, Chairman,
MOI Global

It is truly a privilege to introduce *Hidden Investment Treasures* by Daniel Gladiš. This work stands as a testament to more than three decades of disciplined investing and thoughtful reflection. In the chapters that follow, Daniel shares not only the "what" of selected investments but more importantly the "why"—the reasoning and philosophy behind each decision. Through a series of insightful case studies, he uncovers value in places many investors overlook, much like a patient gardener nurturing saplings into a thriving forest. The result is both a practical guide and a reflective journey into the mind of a seasoned value investor.

Daniel is well-known in global value investing circles as the founder of Vltava Fund and as an author and teacher in the art of investing. Over three decades of market experience, he has earned an impressive long-term track record and the respect of peers worldwide. Daniel's investment philosophy can be described as fundamentally value-oriented, research-driven, and steadfastly focused on the long term. He began his career in the aftermath of Czechoslovakia's transition from communism to a market economy, an experience that shaped his perspective and resilience. Daniel grew up under a communist regime and went on to found one of the Czech Republic's first brokerage firms after the Iron Curtain fell. Having legendary investors like Seth Klarman and Jeremy Grantham as clients inspired Daniel to devote himself to professional investing. This background endowed him with a profound appreciation for economic freedom, prudent risk management, and independent thinking—all of which permeate his approach to investment.

At the core of Daniel's philosophy is the classical value investor's ethos: to buy undervalued, high-quality businesses and hold them patiently as value is realized over time. He does not chase short-term trends or fashions; instead, he diligently seeks out opportunities where price and intrinsic value diverge. As he observes in Chapter 1, broader macroeconomic themes or market noise take a back seat to the specifics of each business he studies. What truly matters to him is the concrete, company-level analysis—understanding a business, its management, its competitive edge, and why the market might be mispricing it. In Daniel's own words, an investment portfolio is ultimately "a collection of individual investments," and what concerns us most is "the specific investments we make and why we make them." This bottom-up focus, combined with a contrarian streak, means he often finds value where others are not looking.

Daniel also emphasizes the importance of patience and long-term thinking, frequently drawing analogies between investing and the slow, steady growth of nature. In the final chapter of the book, he likens the act of picking stocks to planting trees: one cannot see the growth from day to day, but over years the transformation is remarkable. This perspective is a cornerstone of his philosophy—the idea that wealth in the stock market is grown, not manufactured overnight. Daniel is a steadfast believer that time and compounding are an investor's allies. By planting the seeds of investment in well-chosen companies and letting them grow, he has watched small saplings turn into a forest of wealth over the decades. Not every seed will flourish, of course, just as not every stock pick will be a winner. Yet with careful selection, diligent care, and the courage to take a long view, the odds of cultivating a "big and beautiful forest" of investments are greatly enhanced. This patient, almost horticultural approach to investing is a theme Daniel returns to again and again, and it underpins many of the case studies in *Hidden Investment Treasures*.

In Chapter 1, Daniel explains the motivations that led him to write again on investing after a long hiatus. It has been quite a few years since his previous books (*Learn to Invest* in 2004 and *Stock Investing* in 2014) were published, and by his own admission he had thought the book-writing chapter of his life closed. Those earlier works had achieved their goal of educating a generation of Czech investors, and Daniel was content sharing his ongoing insights through quarterly letters to Vltava Fund shareholders. What spurred the creation of *Hidden Investment Treasures* was a recognition that there remained a missing piece in the literature—a comprehensive collection of real-world case studies.

Daniel reflects that whenever he reads other investors' writings or listens to their presentations, the most valuable insights come from concrete examples: specific investments and the reasoning behind them. General discussions of strategy or macroeconomic trends can be informative, but they are ultimately abstract. It is in the particulars—the stories of individual stock picks—that one finds tangible lessons. Realizing this, Daniel set out to write the book he would have loved to read from others: a candid exploration of actual investment ideas, complete with the why and how of each decision.

Another reason for this book is the extraordinary opportunity Daniel sees for value investors in today's market environment. After decades in the markets, he feels that conditions for stock pickers are more favorable now than ever before. Daniel observes a decline in the number of true active investors in recent years, partly due to the rise of passive investing and index funds. Those who remain active and diligent face less competition in uncovering mispriced stocks. He quips that "value investors today must feel like athletes who enter a competition and see that almost no one else is trying to win." The playing field is wide open for those willing to do the work.

Following the introductory chapter, the book unfolds as a series of case-based chapters, each a hunt for hidden value—or as Daniel phrases it, "seeking treasure"—in a different context. These chapters collectively span a remarkable range of industries, geographies, and investment themes.

From iconic large-cap companies to niche sector plays and even entire markets, Daniel demonstrates how a value investor's toolkit can be applied almost anywhere, so long as one remains analytical and discerning.

Each case study in *Hidden Investment Treasures* stands on its own as a lesson. For example, in Chapter 2 on Berkshire Hathaway, Daniel explores the irony of how one of the world's most famous companies can still hide significant value in plain sight. He dissects Berkshire's many moving parts and management's capital allocation mastery, reaffirming why long-term orientation and trust in quality management (as epitomized by Warren Buffett) pay off over decades. In another chapter, Daniel turns to an automotive retailer, Asbury Automotive Group, dubbing it a "cannibal" for its aggressive share buyback strategy. Here readers learn about the power of share repurchases in enhancing per-share value—an oft-underappreciated mechanism for rewarding patient shareholders. Moving through the book, we encounter chapters on companies like Alimentation Couche-Tard, illustrating growth through shrewd acquisitions, and Burford Capital, where the treasure lies in the quality of people and unique business model. Each study is richly detailed, explaining not just the facts of the invest-ment but Daniel's reasoning: What made this opportunity attractive? What risks were weighed? How does it fit into a broader portfolio?

Importantly, these case studies are not mere historical reviews—they are templates for thinking about investments. Daniel generously shares how he evaluates management quality, competitive advantages, capital allocation, and valuation in each situation. Readers gain insight into his analytical process, effectively being mentored in how to spot their own "hidden treasures" in the market. The breadth of examples—from a Swiss alpine railway (Jungfraubahn) to the Japanese Nikkei index, from oil pro-ducers to banks—underscores a key lesson: value investing is a mindset, not a narrow strategy confined to any one sector or region. As Daniel shows, opportunities can be found anywhere if one knows how and where to look. His chapter on Japan, for instance, reveals how an entire country's equity market can become a hidden gem when sentiment and reality diverge; Japan's market, long ignored by global investors, offered such an opportunity with improving corporate governance and low valuations. Through these varied studies, the book highlights the enduring principles of investing—patience, curiosity, and due diligence—while also providing timely insights on today's markets.

The book concludes with a reflective capstone that encapsulates Daniel's investment ethos. This chapter is particularly special: it steps away from analyzing companies and instead shares a personal anecdote that serves as a powerful metaphor for investing. Daniel writes about a piece of land he owns—affectionately nicknamed "Berkshire Park"—where he and his wife have planted trees over the years. His wife tends to the flowers and shrubs, while Daniel focuses on the trees, patiently watching them grow year after year. In this tranquil pastime, Daniel finds an analogy for long-term investing that is as instructive as it is poetic.

He notes that watching a tree grow is not a matter of days or weeks, but of many years. On any given day, progress is imperceptible; yet when one looks back after a decade, one is astonished at how a slender sapling has become a sturdy tree. So it is with investments: "Share price movements are easy to see and often attract attention, but as long-term investors, we are primarily interested in how the company is doing in its business," he writes, reminding us that true value accumulates over time, often out of sight. Just as a forest cannot sprout overnight, a great investment returns value gradually, compounded through the business's growth and prudent management.

Daniel candidly acknowledges that not every tree he planted survived—some died off, due to either mistakes or circumstances beyond control—and likewise not every stock he ever bought turned into a winner. Failure, in both gardening and investing, is a natural part of the process. What matters is that enough of the trees thrived such that, if gathered together, they would form a "big and beautiful forest" of success. In other words, a well-chosen portfolio, tended with care, will yield abundant results even if a few saplings fail. The emphasis is on the process: choose well, nurture your investments, but above all, plant the seeds in the first place. As Daniel concludes, "Stock trees need to be well selected, carefully looked after—but above all they need to be planted. Otherwise, there's nothing to grow." This is a call to action for investors to be proactive and confident in their analysis. One cannot reap the benefits of compounding without first committing capital to opportunities identified as undervalued.

"Berkshire Park" beautifully ties together the themes of the book. It reinforces why Daniel favors active stock selection at a time when many have become passive index investors. He argues that today's market, rife with indiscriminate index flows and algorithmic traders, is increasingly inefficient, creating more mispricings for the patient long-term investor to exploit. The passive approach, while popular, cannot replicate the satisfaction of discovering an overlooked gem and watching it flourish. With the tree-planting metaphor, Daniel leaves readers with a vivid mental image of what true investing feels like: years of quiet growth, occasional setbacks, and the profound reward of seeing one's foresight vindicated over time. The chapter, and the book, thus end on a note of wisdom: value investing is not just a technique, but a temperament—one of patience, diligence, and unwavering optimism in the future.

Beyond his personal investing endeavors and writing, Daniel has been a generous contributor to the broader investment community, notably through MOI Global. As a longstanding member, he has shared insights at various events and platforms dedicated to investor education and idea exchange. I have had the pleasure of interacting with him in these settings and observing first-hand the qualities that make him a standout investor and mentor.

One such forum was Ideaweek St. Moritz, where Daniel's presence left a deep impression on fellow participants. I vividly recall a group discussion in 2018 where Daniel provided fascinating context to his personal path as an investor, reflecting on his formative experiences and philosophy. He spoke of growing up in a planned economy and witnessing the dawn of free markets, of founding a brokerage firm that became the largest in his country, and of his transition into managing an investment fund. These stories, recounted with humility and a touch of humor, underscored Daniel's resilience and adaptive thinking. Despite the vastly different economic environment of his youth, or perhaps because of it, he developed a profound respect for capital and a keen eye for opportunity. At that same Ideaweek session, Daniel delved into aspects of his investment process and shared an idea—his thesis on BMW, describing it as a bargain hiding in plain sight due to the company's strong balance sheet and undervalued assets. The clarity of his analysis and the conviction of his presentation were inspiring to all of us in the room.

Daniel's contributions also extend to The Zurich Project, where he has been part of a select group of asset managers who meet to discuss not just investment ideas but also the business of investing—topics like client relations, fund strategy, and personal development as an investor. In a notable podcast episode from The Zurich Project series, Daniel spoke about "the importance of attracting the right clients" to an investment firm. This might seem an unusual topic for an investment discussion, but it reveals a lot about Daniel's character and long-term orientation. He explained that having patient, like-minded investors in one's fund is "a necessity for long-term survival and success in investment management." In sharing this, Daniel reflected on how he communicates with his clients and sets expectations so that they understand the philosophy of Vltava Fund. Such insight is invaluable to peers: it shows Daniel not only cares about picking the right stocks but also about cultivating the right partnerships with investors. It speaks to his integrity and foresight—he would rather turn away capital than take on investors who might demand short-term results at the expense of long-term performance. This approach has undoubtedly contributed to the enviable track record of his fund, by ensuring he can stick to his strategy through thick and thin.

At MOI Global events, Daniel is known for his thoughtful questions and his willingness to engage with fellow investors, offering guidance without ego. Many, including myself, have benefited from his perspectives. Whether discussing the implications of central bank policies on markets or the nuances of a particular stock idea, Daniel exhibits a remarkable blend of intellect and pragmatism. He has a way of cutting through noise to identify what truly matters—a mental clarity that surely contributes to his investment success. Moreover, he exudes a genuine passion for investing as a craft. It is evident that for Daniel, investing isn't just a job or a means to profits; it is a calling, one that involves continuous learning and sharing of knowledge. His contributions exemplify the collaborative spirit that elevates the investing profession as a whole.

Having known Daniel through these professional circles, I would like to offer a few personal reflections. Daniel is, first and foremost, a person of great integrity. In an industry where short-termism and flashy marketing can tempt even the best, Daniel has remained steadfast to his principles. He values honesty—to himself, to his investors, and to the companies he invests in. This integrity builds trust, which is perhaps why his fund's investors tend to stay with him for the long run, aligned with the journey he maps out. Speaking of journey, Daniel's investment career resembles his impressive journey as an endurance athlete in cross-country skiing, where discipline, determination, and a never-ending quest for knowledge are the prerequisites for great success.

As an investor, Daniel embodies the virtues that define the very best in the field. He is analytical and rigorous, always doing his homework on a company before investing. Readers of this book will see that rigor in the way he dissects the financials and business models in each case study. He is also patient and disciplined—he does not let the allure of quick gains deter him from an approach of measured, compounding growth. In fact, during volatile times, he is often excited rather than fearful, because volatility can bring prices far below intrinsic values (the essence of finding a treasure on sale). I recall conversations during periods of market turmoil where Daniel's calm confidence prevailed; he would say, if we have done our analysis and know what a business is worth, a market panic is the time to invest more, not to panic. This temperament—calm, rational, and opportunistic when others are fearful—is a hallmark of his persona.

On a personal level, Daniel is unfailingly humble and approachable. Despite his accomplishments, he carries himself with the humility of a perpetual student of markets. In group discussions, he is as keen to learn from others' experiences as he is to share his own. This open-mindedness keeps him adaptable. It also makes him a mentor figure to many younger investors. Daniel often says that one of the joys of investing is that it is a continuous learning process; there are always new industries to understand, new global trends to consider, and new mistakes to learn from. Indeed, in one chapter of this book, he openly discusses some investment mistakes (such as in CVS or Microsoft)—a candid willingness to examine what went wrong. Such introspection is evidence of a secure and mature investor, one who learns from every outcome.

Daniel's passion for lifelong learning is evident not only in his writing of this book but in his regular communications. His quarterly letters to shareholders are widely read beyond his fund's client base, as they contain wisdom and commentary on investing that anyone can appreciate. Through his writing and speaking, Daniel has inspired countless individuals to approach the stock market with a rational, value-driven mindset. *Hidden Investment Treasures* is, in a way, the culmination of his learning—a book that distills years of experience into narratives that are accessible, educational, and engaging.

On a lighter note, those of us who have spent informal time with Daniel also know him as a person of warmth and wit. Whether over a dinner in St. Moritz or a coffee break in Zurich, Daniel is quick with a smile and enjoys a good-humored conversation. This personable nature makes the sometimes-daunting subject of investing feel more human. In Daniel's company, one is reminded that investing, at its best, is not about spreadsheets and stock tickers alone but also about life experiences, stories, and relationships. He often draws analogies from history, sports, or forestry to make a point about investing. These reflections show a well-rounded intellect and a man grounded in real life, not just abstract finance.

On these pages, Daniel has opened up his investing playbook and life journey for readers, sharing lessons earned through decades of dedication to the craft. This foreword only scratches the surface of what this book contains. As you turn the pages, you will travel from the "why?" – the very rationale and context behind Daniel's investing journey – to the metaphorical "Berkshire Park," where the long-term fruits of that journey stand tall. You will encounter companies and ideas that span continents and industries, each analyzed through the steady lens of value investing. More importantly, you will see how a seasoned investor thinks, adapts, and remains true to core principles regardless of market fads.

For professional investors, the case studies here offer rich analytical frameworks to apply to your own ideas. For aspiring investors, this book is a masterclass in patience, critical thinking, and independent judgment. Daniel highlights that great investments often lurk in unexpected places – perhaps a "boring" company or an out-of-favor industry – and that one must sometimes dig deep to unearth these gems. His success stories, as well as the occasional missteps candidly described, serve as both inspiration and caution, helping readers calibrate their own decision-making compass.

Allow me to emphasize the timeliness of Daniel's message. In an era where passive investing and algorithm-driven trading command the headlines, Daniel makes a compelling case for the enduring value of active, thoughtful stock picking. He reminds us that the market is ultimately a collection of businesses, not just ticker symbols, and that understanding those businesses can give one an edge that no index fund or machine can replicate. The inefficiencies born of modern market trends are the treasures waiting to be claimed by those with the insight to recognize them. This book equips you with that insight. It is at once a reflective meditation on the investment craft and a practical guidebook filled with actionable wisdom.

I congratulate Daniel on this outstanding contribution to investment literature. Few investors have such a combination of skill, track record, and willingness to share. Fewer still can communicate complex ideas in such an elegant, down-to-earth manner. *Hidden Investment Treasures* is a reflection of its author: insightful, principled, and deeply authentic. I am confident that readers will come away from this book not only with new investment ideas but also with a reinforced appreciation for what it means to invest wisely and well.

It is my hope that as you read this book, you will feel as if you are sitting with Daniel, listening to him recount the tales of his favorite investments and the rationale behind each. Through these pages, may you absorb the lessons of a master investor who has never stopped learning himself. And may those lessons guide you to find your own hidden treasures in the years to come.

Preface

This book has a very unusual form. It consists entirely of individual stock investment ideas. After a foreword beautifully written by John Mihaljevic and an introductory chapter, there follow 15 chapters, each of which presents one of these investment ideas. The thought to write the book in this way came to me quite unexpectedly in May 2024, when I was at the Nordic Value investment conference in Denmark. This conference has the format I like best. It is attended by professional investors, participation is by invitation only, the public has no access to it, and each participant presents one specific stock investment idea. I have several similar conferences on my calendar each year, including Value Spain in Madrid that is organized by Christian Freischütz, Chris Bloomstran's Tulipomania in St. Louis, and John Mihaljevic's online Investment Summits from MOI Global. My Prague Value conference is in the same format. In equities investing, as I prefer and as we practice at our fund, while it is interesting to consider the more general topics concerning investment philosophies and strategies, various macroeconomic perspectives, or debates about trends in economies and around the world, it always comes down ultimately to which specific investments we make and why. That's why I prefer to listen to other investors and their particular investment ideas. This is what adds the greatest and most concrete value.

So, while listening one fine day in May to one of the presentations at Nordic Value, it occurred to me that I would like a book consisting solely of individual stock-picking ideas. I started to think back as to whether I had ever read such a book, but, among perhaps a thousand books on investing and related topics that I had ever read, I could not think of any that were written in this style. I would have loved to read a book describing individual investments while at the same time explaining for each one why the investors had been drawn to make it, what were their reasons for doing so, and how they had gone about analyzing them, but I didn't know of any such book. Gradually, the thought took shape in my mind that maybe I should try to write for myself something that I most look for in other investors. Ever since I was a kid, it has been easy for me to get excited about something, and so while running along the sea near Kronborg Castle on that morning, I would not even have dreamed of ever getting around to writing another book (I considered my writing books to be a matter already settled long ago), and yet by evening I already had sketched out in my head a list of chapters and the main outline of the book and was looking forward to sitting down to start writing when I would be home two days later.

Hidden Investment Treasures therefore describes specific, individual stock investment cases from actual practice. By examining those cases, I demonstrate that today one can find in the markets a whole range of companies whose stock prices are significantly lower than their intrinsic values, whose quality of business is very high, and whose associated risk is often much lower than is the risk of the market as a whole. Fifteen cases are described here. How did I choose them? Certainly not by looking at the returns of various stocks in the markets over the past 5–7 years, identifying those yielding the highest returns, and then retrospectively constructing investment stories around the investment returns making it clear that the stocks should of course have been purchased when they were. Such an approach would have been intellectually shoddy. I picked stocks that we actually bought into Vltava Fund and that we still hold to this day, with the exception of one that has since gone private so we had to sell it. I also tried to make sure that each of the chosen stocks demonstrated a different origin or form of the value we were looking for, that the companies we selected came from various sectors, and that, taken together, they indicated the breadth of opportunities offered in today's markets.

To these 15 selected companies (in 1 case a market index), I then added two additional examples from our portfolio that we regard as investment mistakes. The first is the case of a stock that we never even should have bought, and the second, on the other hand, is an example of a stock that we should not have sold. Even when a person does one's best, sometimes they cannot avoid making an error, and describing mistakes can likewise be useful to the reader.

Although a book like *Hidden Investment Treasures* could be written at any point in time, one of my main reasons to embark on writing it just now is in fact its timeliness. The nature and behavior of the stock markets have changed dramatically over the past few years. This has been driven by the tremendous expansion of passive investing. Among other things, this has brought about a significant reduction in the number of active investors. In more than 30 years of my investment experience, the markets have never seen fewer of them. On one hand, we have a preponderance of passive investors who are not interested in how much an individual stock is worth. This opens up a lot of attractive investment opportunities in parts of the market where the eye of the passive investor cannot see and which most passively invested money avoids. On the other hand, there are fewer and fewer active investors in the markets to seek out these opportunities and profit from them.

Hidden Investment Treasures seeks to address this state of affairs by demonstrating, through individual investment examples, where value can be found in the markets. It aims to show readers how the current nature of stock markets can be understood and used to their advantage. The book could be informative to novice investors as well as investors with many years of experience. I hope that you will enjoy reading this book as much as I enjoyed writing it.

Acknowledgments

To write a book is an intimate and independent undertaking by the author, but one that could not be pursued without the help of many other people. I would like to thank some of them.

First of all, I want to thank my wife, Jarka. Through more than 30 years, she has supported me in all my activities. My writing regimen has involved getting up early in the morning, usually while it was still dark out so that I could write a couple of pages, and then a more than usual absentmindedness through the day as thoughts for how to proceed were taking shape in my head. It's not always easy with me, but I know I can always lean on her. Jarka is also the first and most painstaking reader of everything I write, and she is a very good critic. The book is called *Hidden Investment Treasures*. I discovered my life's greatest treasure when I met Jarka, and I closed the best transaction in my life when I married her. Thank you for everything.

Next, I want to thank everyone who read the manuscript and gave me valuable feedback. Thank you to Petr Čermák, Hana Komárková, Miroslav Koplík, Jiří Kutal, and Jan Žák. Thanks to Gale A. Kirking and Jiří Jež at English Editorial Services for their impeccable translation of the manuscript into English.

I thank my friend John Mihaljevic, founder of MOI Global. John not only has been a good friend and mentor but also has been a longtime strong supporter of me personally and of our fund. Indeed, the main credit must go to him for the fact that John Wiley & Sons, Inc., even considered my manuscript for publication. I am very honored that John took on the task of writing the foreword to the English edition. Thank you.

I thank Bill Falloon, Katherine Cording, and Stacey Rivera at Wiley for their willingness to publish the book and for their work, help, and advice in preparing it for publication.

In the same spirit, I thank a whole lot of other people, both in the investment world and outside of it, who have in one way or another been an inspiration or motivation to me. This list would be extremely long, as well as incomplete, but all of these people are very important to me.

In the end, I must thank also you, the reader, for choosing to pick up this book. Even though I will never know most of you personally, you were a crucial and indispensable part of the motivation for me to sit down and start writing. I hope that you will find inspiration and useful insights in this book. May your investing journeys be filled with success, and may you enjoy the adventure!

Chapter 1

Why?

It has been a while since my previous two books on investing came out. The first edition of *Learn to Invest* was released in 2004, and the first edition of *Stock Investing* was published in 2014. When I think about how many people have written to me since that time saying that these books have helped them to get started in investing, I realize that I could not have wished for anything better and that the two books may well have achieved their primary goal. Even though I have been asked over and over again for more than 20 years when I am going to write another book, I had considered the writing of books to be a closed chapter for me. Both books still sell well, so their contribution and potential are not yet exhausted, and I also didn't want to be among those authors who churn out one thing after another without really having anything new to say. Besides, I write a letter to the shareholders of our investment fund every quarter. It's also available to the public and has a very large readership from all over the world, and I see it as a kind of open book on a continuing basis. So, no more books. I was very clear on that point, and I believed it for a long time. On the other hand, I knew that when I read something that other investors write, or when I follow what they say, what they present at various investment conferences and so on, I'm always most interested in their particular investments and the reasons that led them to make these. In the stock investing that I prefer and that we also practice at Vltava Fund, while the more general topics concerning investment philosophies and strategies, various macroeconomic views, or debates about trends in economies and in the world as a whole are interesting, what ultimately concerns us when all is said and done is always the specific investments we make and why we make them.

An investment portfolio is a collection of individual investments. Among the tens of thousands of possibilities available to investors in the markets, we must find our way to each of these individually. We need to find them, understand them, analyze them, value them, determine the level and types of their associated risks, and then be able to compare them against one another in order to select the few that will be included into the portfolio. This occurs over and over and over again. Consisting as it does of a search for individual stocks, such an approach to investing necessarily is dominated by factors specific to each company under consideration. What is its type of business, the level and sustainability of its competitiveness, the quality of its management, the probability with which its future fate and potential can be predicted, its risk, and, of course, the relationship between its share price and its intrinsic value? Broader themes, such as the state of the economy and its growth, the ups and downs of individual sectors, inflation, interest rates, currency risk, and so forth have rather marginal influence in the selection of individual investments. Therefore, what always interests me most about other investors are their specific investments and, most of all, if they can explain the rationale behind each of them. Seeking out this information provides me the greatest added value and the best opportunity to continue learning.

Up until now, I have not written a book that would both describe our individual investments and, for each one of them, explain why we made it, what were our reasons, and how we went about analyzing it. A thought began gradually taking shape in my mind that maybe I should try to write for myself something that I look for most from other investors. Psychologists might say that I have open shapes in my head. While it is true that I always describe my reasons for each investment in the Vltava Fund on an ongoing basis through my letters to shareholders, they could be better detailed in a book and made seamlessly available to readers in a single place.

Also contributing to my decision finally to take the plunge and start writing is the fact that the market environment for selecting individual stock investments is better today for value investors than it ever has been through the entirety of my investing lifetime. I started investing in the spring of 1993, and since that time I've been in the markets uninterruptedly every day. Indeed, in all those 31 years, the conditions for selecting individual stock investments have never been more favorable than they are now. How is that possible? The simple answer is that it's because there are fewer investors trying to do so. That means the level of competition among those investors is less and so they have the entire wide field open to themselves. There has never been anything like it before. Value investors today must feel like athletes who enter a competition and see that almost no one else is trying to win. They scarcely could ask for anything more.

Let me try to explain two things that are important for understanding the overall situation. I first will explain conceptually what a value investor is, and then I will describe how it could be that so few of them remain and why that is almost a godsend for them.

How We Got to This Point

Investment literature sometimes tries to classify investors into groups according to their investment strategies. Then it talks about investors who profess strategies known as growth, value, growth at a reasonable price (GARP), momentum, dividend, income, contrarian, socially responsible, activist, and I don't know what all else. I never really liked this categorization because it is too vague. The different classifications do not have precise definitions, sometimes they overlap, and some of the names can be misleading. This is precisely the case for value investing strategies. Value investing is often described as a strategy whereby investors buy stocks that have low P/Es (price to earnings, which is the ratio of share price to earnings per share) or have low P/BVs (price to book, which is the ratio of share price to book value per share), stocks in companies that are not growing much and that tend to be more established and stable businesses. Growth investment strategies are often presented in contrast to value, with these investors typically characterized as looking for younger and sometimes smaller companies that have above-average growth potential and so they are willing to pay higher prices for their shares.

Value investing as we understand it, and as it should be interpreted, is not related to what earnings multiples an investor is willing to pay or whether they prefer more established and stable companies versus companies with rapid growth. Value investing means that the investor is consistently careful to buy shares at prices that are lower than their value. The expected growth of a company always plays an important role in estimating value, and value investors can buy any stock if they can demonstrate to themselves through rigorous analysis that the ratio of price to value is attractive. The fact that a company is growing rapidly does not automatically mean that its value also is growing. One can find many examples of rapidly growing companies wherein that growth is literally destroying value. On the flip side, there is no automatic guarantee that companies whose shares trade at low earnings multiples will be good investments. Again, there are plenty of examples where nominally cheap stocks have turned out to be so-called "value traps." No stock can be rejected or accepted simply on the basis of whether it trades at low or high multiples of earnings or of cash flows or based upon whether the company is growing fast or slow. In all cases, an attempt should be made to estimate the intrinsic value of the company and then to compare this with the share price. In our understanding, this is true value investing. At Vltava Fund, we consider ourselves value investors, but, if you look at what we hold, our portfolio is made up almost exclusively of growth companies. There is no contradiction in this. We define a growth company for our purposes as one whose intrinsic value is increasing at a rate of at least 10% per year. Such a growth rate is well above average compared to the stock market as a whole. Some investors, including some of the greatest legends in the business, even say that all investing is value investing, because all investing must necessarily be striving to buy investments at prices below their intrinsic values. Any other approach, they say, should not be called investing at all. I definitely am inclined toward that view. It makes a lot of sense to me and applies to all types of investment, not just stock investments.

Then why are there so few value investors these days? Market developments in recent years, and especially an upsurge in passive investing, have contributed to this. All stock market participants can be divided into active and passive. Active investors seek out individual stock opportunities for investment according to their individual attractiveness and then construct their portfolios around these. Passive investing is the polar opposite of active investing. It does not strive to select individual investments. Passive investors are not really interested in how much a stock is worth or how much they pay for it, because they put their money into investment instruments that by their composition replicate some index. These are most often index funds or exchange-traded funds (ETFs). Indices are constructed by various methods. Most of these combine subjective rules drawn up by the people who create the index with automatic calculations that often take into account how much a stock costs and what its market capitalization is. Ironically, perhaps, passive investors, who are not interested in individual stocks and are wholly indifferent as to their cost within the index, rely upon the actions of active investors who, by seeking out individual attractive investments, maintain a process known as *price discovery*. This is how a stock's price is determined together with what representation it will then have in the various indices. Passive investors cannot invest without the existence of active investors. They are dependent upon them. An index is not some market-independent and objective measure of market performance. Its composition changes depending on the development of the market itself, which is to say, depending upon the very thing that it is supposed to be measuring. Moreover, it is influenced by the decisions of a committee within the company that compiles and manages the index.

Price Discovery and Market Trends

If there were only a few passive investors in the markets and a majority were in fact active investors and if the process of price discovery were relatively fast and efficient, then even passive investors could consider the composition of the indices in which they invest and the concentrations of the largest stocks within those indices to be fair. Unfortunately, however, we long ago abandoned this reality. As early as 2019, analyses began to emerge showing that more than 50% of the total amount of money managed in the U.S. market is invested passively. These investments are in a variety of index funds and ETFs, as well as in other retail, pension, and institutional index-linked products. We must also include among these passive investments money in seemingly active funds that may outwardly appear to be active but that are in fact almost entirely passive.

If we had already exceeded the 50% mark for passively invested money in 2019, then we are surely well beyond that today as the process of shifting money into passive funds is rapidly continuing. We could very well be at 60%. It might seem that having 40% of the money remaining among active investors is enough to provide reasonably efficient and rapid price discovery. A further problem, however, is that not all of this money is invested such that it participates in the price-discovery process. First of all, we need to subtract from this amount those shares that, although not invested in passive strategies, are also not traded at all. These are the ownership stakes of major shareholders. In the largest companies having the greatest representation in the indices and to which therefore flow sizable sums of passively invested money, key shareholders often own large proportions of the shares. These are companies such as Alphabet, Meta, Berkshire Hathaway, and Tesla. Although these shares are formally classified as actively traded, they are not really on the market and scarcely are traded at all. In these companies, therefore, only somewhere around 20% can be regarded as actively managed money. And even this small proportion of shares still is not invested such that it ensures an efficient price-discovery process. Indeed, this part of the market includes money from investors who do not try to look for disparities between price and value. These include, for example, investors devoted to momentum strategies, various forms of algorithmic trading, or technical analysis. It also includes small retail investors, the vast majority of whom have neither financial education nor skills necessary to conduct fundamental analysis of individual companies. Any contribution from all these types of investors to effective price discovery is limited.

In fact, it could even be said that the boom in passive investing has reached such a point that passive investors have ceased to be so-called price takers and have become their own active price makers. This is a result of how money flows in the markets. When money flows into passive funds and ETFs, the funds automatically use it to buy stocks. (More on the workings of ETFs in a later chapter.) They hold almost no cash but immediately put it into those stocks and in such proportions as prescribed by the current composition of the index they replicate. By the very nature of things, if new money is flowing into passive funds, their purchases must be satisfied by selling from active investors. However, these investors are becoming increasingly scarce in relative terms and their willingness to sell must logically be balanced by ever higher share prices. If we take this situation to the absurd in our imagination, then, with the magnitude of passive investors increasingly outweighing that of active investors, share prices will have to rise exponentially as passive investors continue to buy, because the marginal price required to meet demand from an ever-smaller supply of sellers must rise ever faster. The price paid to the last existing active investor should theoretically be infinite.

If the situation reverses and money starts flowing out of passive funds, then the impact on share prices will be the opposite and again very considerable. The only people who could absorb a massive sell-off of passive funds would be active investors. They, however, do not have nearly enough cash for that purpose. On average, active investors hold maybe something like 5% of their portfolios in cash. Five percent of the 20% of total assets held by active investors is only about 1% of the amount of money in the markets. This is the amount of cash that theoretically could be called upon to hold back a tsunami of money rolling out of passive funds. Of course, added to this still would be money residing outside the stock markets but that could move into them, such as money coming from the companies themselves through share buybacks, or money held in bond funds, for example, but the willingness of those holding this capital to bail out falling share prices, and especially a willingness to react quickly, would very likely be negligible. Active investors would be about equally unwilling to try and shore up the market, notwithstanding the fact that they would be unable to do so in any case with the limited free cash at their disposal.

Just as an enormous predominance of buying by passive funds could theoretically push shares prices to infinity, so, too, could a large preponderance of selling ultimately cause prices to fall nearly to zero. Now, I'm aware that expressions like infinity and zero are in the case of share prices just turns of phrase to describe extreme and improbable situations that will not occur, but they nevertheless suggest the direction that share prices will take when there is a huge prevalence of passively invested money over active money and if the flows of money into or out of passive funds behave as I have depicted them. I think one can find many instances in the markets of extremely large movements, either of the whole index or, more often up to now, of individual stocks, which are driven by changes in the flows of money into passive funds.

To illustrate how passive investors are gradually moving from being share price takers to share price makers, or perhaps better said comakers, it is necessary to consider the impact that the flows of money into passive funds have on the composition of the very indices that they replicate. While active investors, when selecting stocks, are interested in whether a stock is trading at 5 times earnings, 50 times earnings, or even 100 times earnings, passive investors couldn't care less. They buy stocks regardless of their individual valuations according to what the current composition of the index prescribes. The weights of the shares in each index are largely influenced by the market capitalizations of the individual companies. This is logical. The larger a company's market capitalization, the bigger the part of the overall market it represents and the more weight it deserves in the index composition. In a world where there are plenty of active investors in the markets and where valuations of individual companies tend relatively well to reflect the fundamental values of individual companies, the composition of indices would be determined with the same degree of efficiency. If, however, the quantity of passively invested money far outweighs that of actively invested money, then much of the price discovery will be in the hands of passive investors. That is to say, prices will be governed by those investors who do not engage in any analysis of individual stocks, have no idea of their intrinsic values, and, when buying or selling them, do not really care about their individual share prices. Be that as it may, their investments do have a significant impact on those prices.

In addition to an enormous number of index funds and ETFs on the markets, there exist also many individual indices. Indices can represent entire markets, but also individual sectors, regions, strategies, and so on. They influence each other in their composition based on how much passively invested money flows into the various indices, and a gradual change in the composition of the indices in turn influences which stocks get more and which get less money. Stocks, sectors, or regions whose weightings in the indices are increasing attract growing proportions of passive investment, which, in turn, drives their weightings in the indices even higher. A greater weighting in the indices then means an even larger share of new money, and thus again higher weightings in the indices, and so on and so forth. Feedback loops work very well here. An active investor who analyzes and follows hundreds of individual companies can see clearly how the price-discovery process is disrupted and distorted by the dominance of passive investing. That is especially the case if they can compare the change as it occurs over time. An investor exclusively using passive investment, on the other hand, has no way of assessing this situation at all.

Ultimately then, as money flows toward passive funds, there is a growing concentration of the largest titles in the indices (currently the highest in history, surpassing even the Nifty Fifty bubble of the 1960s).

When money flows reverse, exiting from passive funds, then it is the stocks with the largest representation in the indices that take the worst beating, because their prices are most affected by the insufficiency of buyers from active funds. Here again, the feedback loop works very well. An example may be seen in the U.S. market during 2022. It was then that the largest stocks in the indices performed the worst. This is illustrated by the performance at that time of the seven stocks that were collectively nicknamed "The Magnificent Seven" (M7). These companies are Alphabet, Amazon, Apple, Meta, Microsoft, Nvidia, and Tesla. Over the course of 2022, these stocks collectively declined by 40.2%. When we break down their stock price movements into their smaller components, we find that over the course of 2022, the M7's earnings per share declined by 8.7%, their sales per share grew by 10.1%, and their profit margins fell by 17.1%. Significantly, their P/E contracted by a full third – from a starting level of 38.4× to an ending level of 25.1×. (All of this and more is discussed in beautiful detail in the 2023 Letter to Clients from Semper Augustus Investment Group.) The 40% share price decline of the M7 was much greater than the 19.4% decline in the S&P 500 index. It is likely that this resulted largely from there simply being neither enough willingness in the minds of active investors nor sufficient money available in their pockets to absorb the sell-off from passive funds. This was most pronounced in those stocks having the largest representations in the index. The prices of these stocks then had to fall substantially to bring supply and demand into balance.

The year 2023, then, brought a beautiful reversal of 2022. Money flow turned once again toward passive funds, and, just as in the year previous there had not been enough active investors in the markets to absorb the sales of passive funds, in 2023 there were not sufficient stocks in the hands of active investors on offer for passive investors to buy. Thus, while the S&P 500 index rose by 24.2% in 2023, the M7 stocks gained 75.8%. This growth was mostly driven by increases in earnings per share (35.8%), sales per share (12%), margins (21.2%), and P/E (29.7%). In the 2 years combined, M7 share prices rose by 4.7% while the S&P 500 index rose by just 0.07%.

The large proportion of passive investors in the markets has a tendency to prolong and accentuate trends that are emerging in the markets – in entire broad indices, in individual market segments, and in individual stocks. This occurs in both directions, when the market is going up and when it is falling. **Overall, then, there arises a paradoxical situation wherein the indices that should be the benchmarks for performance become themselves the investment target and thus actually cease to be good benchmarks.** And all of this is because of the money flows from investors who are not concerned at all with the valuation of individual stocks.

Why?

Now, I should note that I did not write this book to criticize passive investing. That is not at all my intention. I do not consider the idea of passive investing in and of itself to be a bad one. On the contrary, it's a useful thing that is or can be convenient for many different types of investors. Moreover, passive investing should not be regarded as engaging in some sort of competition with active investing. Passive and active investing are not mutually exclusive. Investors can use both at the same time in various combinations, and it's good to remember that passive investing itself necessarily involves a number of active decisions that the investor has to make. After all, even we at Vltava Fund, as you will see later, use a passive investing option for one particular investment position, and yet we see ourselves as quite orthodox active investors. It is also important that the overriding mission of an investor is not to criticize something. An investor should not invest according to what they wish would happen or how they would like the world to look but, rather, consistent with what they think will actually happen. These are usually two very different things, and it doesn't do us any good to mix them up.

This book was written for a different reason. Everything, no matter how good the idea, has its negative consequences. Those impacts often run counter to the original intent. The more extreme an original idea and its application, the more pronounced the side effects can be. The rate of passive investing's expansion is quite unprecedented. There has never been anything like it before. The effects on the functioning and behavior of markets are also unprecedented. This is something that investors should understand and be well aware of, adapt to, and, ideally, make use of. The environment that has taken shape here is completely new and has created a great opportunity for active investors. If I could choose for myself what I would most appreciate in markets so that we active investors could invest well in them, then I would wholeheartedly welcome a situation wherein the majority of investors are not concerned about what they are buying and at what price, instead leaving that to a handful of active investors. As a person who has been involved in sports and racing all my life, I would relish a situation where almost none of the competitors is trying to be the best and almost all of them give up before they even start. We are very close to that state of affairs in the markets today. Ten, twenty, thirty years ago, the competition in the markets to find individual investments was much tougher than it is today. Back then, active investors were not presented the kind of favorable environment that they are now.

Active and value investing is based on a view that the theory of perfectly efficient markets is wrong. Any validity of this theory is constructed upon several assumptions. Investor access to the market must be free, the cost of acquiring information must be minimal, and there must be a highly competitive investment environment. It is the degree of this competition that is significantly reduced by the large scale of passive investing. Markets are becoming less elastic and less price sensitive. In a highly competitive and price-elastic environment, investors would sell stocks whose prices have risen too high because their expected returns would be too low and would instead buy stocks whose prices were at more attractive levels. However, as I described, passive investors automatically buy just what the composition of the indices prescribes, regardless of whether individual stocks are cheap or expensive. The low liquidity caused by the declining representation of active investors in the markets creates bottlenecks making it difficult to balance supply and demand. Because markets are becoming less and less price elastic, they require larger and larger price reactions. Index investing is entirely founded on the assumption that markets are efficient even as that very process itself is reducing their efficiency. Passive investors have gone from being price takers to price makers. Even Jack Bogle himself, the founder of the Vanguard Group and the greatest pioneer and popularizer of index investing, said near the end of his life that if all investors used index investing, "chaos, catastrophe" could be expected, and the markets would fail (Udland, 2017). We will never get to a point where all investors use passive investing exclusively. The markets would have collapsed much earlier than that. Nonetheless, with today's significant preponderance of passively managed money over active money, the functioning of the markets is significantly impaired, and much more so than ever before.

An intelligent investor will not only get off this passive investing train but will use the whole situation to their advantage. Provided that active investors come to grips with the new state of the markets, understand how and in what ways market behavior has changed, and adjust their own investing, including their own expectations, they stand a good chance of having their portfolios provide returns higher than those of the broad markets while bearing much less risk than that of the broad markets.

What to Expect in the Remainder of This Book

The remaining chapters of this book describe individual investment cases from practice. Using case studies, I aim to demonstrate that one can find a whole range of stocks in the markets today that are priced significantly below their values, represent high-quality businesses, and often have associated risk much lower than that of the overall market. Described here are 15 case studies in total. Various lengths of text are devoted to each. Some require more extensive description while others can be and are much shorter. In selecting the individual investments, I have also endeavored to consider that the investment rationale for each should include some more general investment theme transferable to other companies and that holds true over the long term.

How did I select the individual cases? That determination most certainly was not made by looking at the returns of various stocks in the markets over the past 5–7 years, identifying those yielding the highest returns, and then retrospectively constructing investment stories around the investment returns making it clear that the stocks should of course have been purchased then and there. I picked stocks that we actually bought into Vltava Fund and that we still hold to this day, with the exception of one that has since gone private (Teekay Energy Partners) and so we had to sell it. I also tried to make sure that each of the chosen stocks demonstrated a different origin or form of the value we were looking for, that the companies we selected came from various sectors, and that, taken together, they indicated the breadth of opportunities that today's markets offer. To these 15 selected companies (in one case a market index), I then added two additional examples from our portfolio that we regard as investment mistakes. The first is the case of a stock that we never even should have bought, and the second, by contrast, is an example of a stock that we should not have sold. Even when a person does one's best, sometimes they cannot avoid making an error. The advantage then is that they have something at hand from which to learn for the rest of one's investment life. The fact that only one of these 15 companies is based in the EU is not by design, but, unfortunately, it does reflect a little of the relative decline in the importance of the region we live in.

I have tried to explain everything in as simple terms as possible. There exists a lot more work behind the individual cases than could be shown here, and that, after all, is not the aim of the book. This book is not a standard investment analysis or a set of investment tips. An aim is to make it understandable also to novice investors who have only a few years of experience and to help them along their way through the world of stocks.

Before we delve into the individual investment cases, let me make one small comment. This text so far has focused on the U.S. market. This is not because I want to ignore other markets. It is because the U.S. market is by far the largest in the world. It currently accounts for approximately 60% of the world stock market capitalization and has a similar representation in various global stock indices. It is also the market within which the largest proportion of investors invest, it is the most developed, and it is the most investable. Its returns will of course not always be better than those of other markets, but almost certainly it will always command the top position for investor attention. The U.S. market is also that market where passive investing has probably advanced furthest, and it is a very broad market wherein the overall composition of the indices is not too much influenced by a few individual companies whose sizes are completely out of line with the rest of the local stock market. In such markets, the concentration of large stocks in the indices is even greater than in the United States, but this is largely due to reasons other than the expansion of passive investing. For example, countries such as Switzerland (due to Nestlé, Novartis, and Roche), France (thanks to LVMH Moët Hennessy, L'Oréal, and Hermés), Denmark (mainly because of Novo Nordisk) and, of course, the Czech Republic (due to CEZ) have high concentrations of the largest companies in the index. India, Japan, and China are examples of markets having lower concentrations than does the United States.

This book was written in the summer of 2024. When I finished writing it, I unified the share prices, returns, and data for each company with reference to the end of September 2024, unless otherwise stated. I submitted the manuscript to the publisher during October to prepare it for printing, and anything that happened later in the markets or in individual stocks can no longer be reflected in the text.

We will now launch into the individual investment cases and examples of where one may seek treasures in the stock markets.

Chapter 2

Berkshire Hathaway

Seeking Treasure in a Company Whose Success Has for Decades Been Playing Out Right in Front of Us

Berkshire Hathaway is a name familiar to a sizable proportion of the public, including even to people who do not themselves invest at all and despite that the company itself does not really produce anything. It is a huge conglomerate of companies that of course individually offer products and services, but people often don't even know that these firms are owned by Berkshire Hathaway. They know Berkshire because it is one of the most successful companies in American – and indeed global – history. Its successful run has spanned six decades and has been led by the investment legend Warren Buffett. When Warren Buffett acquired control of the company and took its helm in May 1965, its shares were priced at $18 apiece. Today, they cost $691,000. Under

Buffett's management and in his hands, the market value of Berkshire's stock has grown more than 38,000-fold. A staggering number. Yet, Buffett did not originally intend to take over Berkshire at all, and a few years earlier even had wanted to sell all of its shares.

How did it all come about? At some point during 1962, Buffett had begun gradually buying Berkshire stock as a regular portfolio investment into Buffett Partnership Limited, an entity where he had managed his clients' money along with his own since 1956. In 1965, he had wanted to sell all of the Berkshire shares and in fact had agreed with then Berkshire President Seabury Stanton to sell. They had settled on a price of $11.50, and the buyer was to be Berkshire Hathaway itself. But, when Buffett received the formal selling offer in the mail, the price was shown as $11.375. One-eighth of $1 lower. This apparently angered Buffett, because, as they say, "a deal is a deal" and should be honored. He did a 180-degree turn in his intentions and began aggressively snapping up the stock. Eventually, he had so many shares that, with the help of some other shareholders, he was able to take control of Berkshire and become its chairman and CEO.

From Zero to a Trillion Dollars

He was now at the head of a company that wasn't worth much at the time. It was a textile enterprise with roots going back to the nineteenth century, but it was a rather subpar business. In the decade leading up to Buffett's takeover, Berkshire's sales had been falling, its financial position was weakening, and it was under increasing competitive threat from cheap Asian goods. Even by the standards of the time, this was a rather small company. Annual sales were around $50 million and equity about $22 million. But Buffett viewed Berkshire Hathaway as an investment vehicle through which he intended to reinvest capital. Once he had done a little digging, Buffett began to look for more attractive and efficient places in which to deploy the capital that the still-profitable textile business was then generating. The first major move that signaled Buffett's intentions came in 1967, when he bought the National Indemnity insurance company, including its affiliate National Fire & Marine, for $8.6 million.

Buffett had long had a close relationship with the insurance business and understood it very well. That's why he also realized the value an insurance company could have in the hands of a good investor and owner. Through their activities, insurance companies create so-called "float." This is an amount of money that insurers hold internally and that is earmarked for payment of future claims. Technically, these funds do not belong to the company and are therefore reported as a liability on their balance sheets. The income generated by investing the float, however, does belong to the insurance company. This float arises due to the time difference between when the insurer collects premia for the policies it sells and when it pays out any claims related to those insurance policies. Depending on the type of insurance, the difference between these two events can range from a few weeks to several decades. In the meantime, the insurance company can make use of the money for its own benefit. How it does so is not entirely arbitrary, because the insurer needs to be sure that it will actually have the money when the time comes to pay out according to the policy, but the proceeds still belong to it. Most insurance companies have the bulk of their float invested in bonds, precisely so that the invested principal is at minimal risk. The returns on insurance companies' bond portfolios are respectable but not earth-shattering.

Buffett may have had a different long-term vision from the beginning. Jumping forward more than six decades to the present, and it is the insurance group that represents the greatest value within the entire Berkshire Hathaway conglomerate. It has been able over time to build a float that today stands at $170 billion, and because Berkshire's insurance companies have a huge surplus of capital relative to the size of their insurance business, this allows them to invest a large portion of that float in stocks over the long term. Even if stock markets were dramatically to decline, as has happened several times over the years, Berkshire need not fear that its capitalization and the business itself, including the ability to pay its claims, would be threatened. The long-term returns on equities are far greater than those on bonds or other underlying asset classes, and Berkshire shareholders have fully benefited from this. It is possible that Buffett had this vision in mind already back in 1967, but he himself probably had no idea how huge the entire float would eventually become.

The year 1967 thus marked the start of the insurance business within the conglomerate as a whole, the beginning of building the float, and the origination of another source of capital that could be continuously reinvested. Not only was Buffett a pioneer who understood how the insurance companies' float could be used to build value over the long term, he also had two other indispensable qualities: he was a good investor, and he had ample patience. The latter is absolutely crucial, because things move relatively slowly in this type of business. Even a decade after Buffett took the helm at Berkshire, the entire conglomerate as a whole had revenues of only about $100 million, equity of $88 million, and float of $79 million.

As capital within Berkshire grew over time, more and more acquisitions were made, they got bigger and bigger, and the acquired businesses themselves began to contribute to further and faster capital growth. Among those that were crucial for their time, I would include the acquisitions of Illinois National Bank & Trust of Rockford (1969, $17 million), See's Candies (1972, $25 million), Buffalo News (1977, $35 million), Nebraska Furniture Mart (1983, $60 million), Scott Fetzer (1986, $410 million), Flight Safety (1996, $1.5 billion), the half of GEICO it did not already own (1996, $2.3 billion), General Reinsurance Corporation (1998, $22 billion), MidAmerican Energy Holdings (2000, 75% for $2 billion), Clayton Homes (2003, $1.7 billion), ISCAR (2006, 80% for $4 billion), Burlington Northern Santa Fe (2010, $44 billion), Lubrizol (2011, $9.7 billion), Precision Castparts (2016, $37 billion), Pilot Flying J (in two parts, 2017 and 2023), and Alleghany Corporation (2022, $11.6 billion) (Mead, 2021).

There were many more transactions, and there is no need to mention them all here. The ones I've listed give a pretty good picture of how the company's capital snowballed over time. In parallel with these private company acquisitions, Buffett invested and reinvested another large sum of money in publicly traded shares. This portfolio (including the portion held in cash) today totals approximately $600 billion. The largest stock positions include Apple, Bank of America, American Express, Coca-Cola, Chevron, Occidental Petroleum, and Kraft Heinz. Berkshire Hathaway's market capitalization hit $1 trillion for the first time in the summer of 2024.

Today, Berkshire Hathaway is a huge conglomerate that for simplicity's sake can be divided into two halves. One is an investment portfolio made up of publicly traded companies and cash, and the other is a group of more than 100 private companies in which Berkshire has ownership stakes. That ownership is often 100%, but not always. In the private part, most valuable is the insurance group, followed by the BNSF railroad, a group of energy companies collectively called Berkshire Hathaway Energy, and then a whole range of other manufacturing and services companies. The individual subsidiaries have almost absolute functional autonomy and management. While the conglomerate as a whole employs almost 400,000 people, only a small group work at Berkshire Hathaway's headquarters in Omaha. I'd estimate they total at most 30 employees. Warren Buffett, as CEO, then makes key decisions in two areas with regard to the subsidiaries: management remuneration and allocation of the earned capital. That is to say, how much money each subsidiary retains each year for its own further development and acquisitions and how much is instead sent up to conglomerate headquarters, making it available to Buffett for other and more efficient uses.

In addition to Buffett, there are four key figures in the top management of the conglomerate: Greg Abel, Ajit Jain, Todd Combs, and Ted Weschler. Greg Abel will become CEO of Berkshire after Buffett's departure. He has already taken over a large part of Buffett's activities and duties. Abel is responsible for the entire private part of the conglomerate, and, when he becomes CEO, he'll be adding another big role. That will be to oversee allocation of the other part of Berkshire that is invested in publicly traded stocks. That investment portfolio will be managed by a pair of investment managers, Todd Combs and Ted Weschler. Each has already been managing a portion of this portfolio for more than 10 years. Greg Abel will still be standing above them and presumably will decide how much of the assets will be kept in the public portion and how much will be kept in the private portion. The most valuable part of the conglomerate, the insurance companies, is now run by Ajit Jain.

Is Berkshire Hathaway a Good Business?

The question then presents itself: is Berkshire Hathaway a good business? We can answer that both philosophically and numerically. From a philosophical perspective, it unambiguously is a good business. Berkshire Hathaway is a collection of generally above-average enterprises crowned by a jewel that is the insurance companies. The insurance group is the best, strongest, and largest insurance business in the world. It has unprecedented capital strength and a matchless market position. It produces a huge float that can be invested largely in equities over the long term to achieve high returns on capital. The float can be thought of essentially as a loan with infinite maturity and a negative interest rate. It constitutes huge added value. Capital allocation at the level of the overall conglomerate is brilliant. It benefits both from Buffett's investment skills and from certain tax advantages that allow capital to be moved efficiently across the conglomerate. Berkshire's financial strength is immense. It currently has nearly $300 billion in cash and very little debt. This gives it both resilience and stability, plus flexibility in times of crisis. The interests of management are well aligned with those of other shareholders. All five key individuals mentioned have substantial portions of their own wealth invested in Berkshire stock. Moreover, they did not receive these shares – as is common in other companies – through management bonuses or option schemes. Rather, they had to buy them with their own money. The same can be said of the members of the board of directors. All of this is then reflected in the managerial mindset, which is very long-term in its orientation and entirely focused on value creation. Berkshire's business culture could serve as a model for all other firms.

That all sounds nice, but it would be just empty words if they weren't backed up by numbers. Let's take a look at some basic figures. If we were to base our analysis on the movement of Berkshire's share price over the period that Warren Buffett has been at the helm, since 1965, then there would be really nothing more to discuss. The stock's returns are so incredibly high that they beat not only the stock markets but also any other comparison. The outperformance of the S&P 500 index is so great that, as noted by my friend and investor Christopher Bloomstran, who has a phenomenally detailed knowledge of Berkshire, the share price could fall by 90% today and still outperform the index during the time under Buffett's leadership. But what happened in the decades before we bought Berkshire stock is of little relevance to us as investors. How have the shares performed since January 2012, when they first appeared in Vltava Fund's portfolio? At the time, they were priced at $119,000. Today, at the end of September 2024, their price stands at $691,180, having grown by 4.8 times. The S&P 500 index has moved from an initial value of 1,312 to the current 5,762 over the same period and has therefore risen by 3.4 times. So, Berkshire is performing better by this measure as well.

A stock's price, however, is not the same as its value, and on its own price often doesn't say much about the quality of a business. In fact, there are two basic components blended into the share price – one fundamental and one psychological. The fundamental takes into account the intrinsic value of the company, and the psychological reflects what price the market is currently willing to pay for that value. Put simply, we can write that the share price (P) is equal to the earnings per share (EPS) times the price/earnings multiple (P/E) that the market is willing to pay for those earnings (i.e., $P = EPS \times P/E$). Over a long investment horizon, we can assume that the share price tends to converge upon the intrinsic value of the company and that its price change over the long term is also close to the long-term change in the company's value. In the medium term, and especially in the short term, the price may also move in a way that is unrelated to the intrinsic value of the company and its development. The price then is more in the grip of market psychology and the flow of money in the markets. So, if we want to judge the quality of a business, we do so not by the movement of its share price but by what are its returns on capital, free cash flows, and profits, for example, as well as by how these values develop over time.

If we were to compare the quality and growth of Berkshire Hathaway and the quality and growth of the companies in the S&P 500 on the basis of the simplest indicator, profitability, then the comparison would be as follows. At the end of 2011, just before we bought Berkshire stock, our earnings per share estimate was $11,100. I say "estimate" deliberately, because the official accounting profitability reported by the company itself differs from that number, and often quite significantly. Sometimes it's higher, sometimes it's lower. Also, analyses from brokerage firms usually show incorrect numbers. This is because of a number of factors, and therefore a few adjustments are needed to arrive at the actual profitability. In September 2024, our earnings per share estimate (still calculated using the same method) was $49,000. The earnings per share therefore increased by 3.4 times. Earnings per share for companies included in the S&P 500 index have grown from an initial $86.90 to the current $202 over the comparable period, according to S&P Global data, and thus by only 1.3 times. Berkshire Hathaway's book value, which in its case is also a good indicator of value and especially its change over time, has increased by 3.2 times over the period from an initial $99,860 to the current $420,000. The growth in book value is almost identical to the growth in earnings per share.

Berkshire's seemingly boring and conservative business is in fact growing much faster than the companies in the index. The S&P 500 index has lagged Berkshire's share price performance over these more than

12 years, even though it has become much more expensive over that time. At the end of 2011, the index was trading at a reasonable P/E of 15.1× and in September 2024 at a very high P/E of 28.4×. Berkshire shares have also become more costly, but not by so much. The price to book value has moved from 1.2× to 1.6×. Despite their price outperformance relative to the index, Berkshire shares are in fact a bit cheaper today relative to that index and in value terms than they were at the beginning of 2012. We expect them not only to outperform the index again over the next decade, but very likely to beat it by an even greater margin. And through all of this, Berkshire's business risk is lower than that of the index. Among large U.S. companies, Berkshire clearly has the lowest business risk for reasons I have outlined. Thus, paradoxically, Berkshire Hathaway stock provides a combination of above-average return and below-average risk. According to efficient markets theory, this combination is something that cannot even exist. The theory argues that higher return must be balanced by greater risk. But that's not true – it doesn't. To illustrate how fast Berkshire's business is growing, Figure 2.1 shows the development of Berkshire's book value per share and that of earnings per share for companies in the S&P 500 since 2011. Both measures are converted to the same basis.

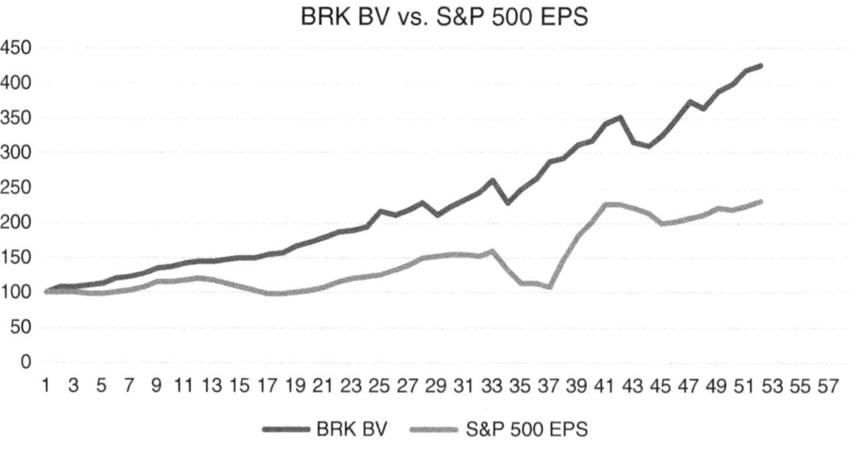

Figure 2.1 Growth in Berkshire Hathaway's book value per share and the S&P 500 index's earnings per share.
Sources: S&P Global and Berkshire Hathaway.

Berkshire Hathaway's Intrinsic Value

Just because something is growing faster is not in and of itself a reason for investing. Moreover, growth alone also is not a reason to invest. Growth does not necessarily create value. It can also destroy value. Moreover, even a rapidly growing company whose growth does create value need not be a good investment. In fact, we are missing another essential piece of information in the overall equation, and that is the share price. For every share there exists a price level at which it is expensive, a price level at which it is inexpensive, and, logically, an approximate price level at which it is correctly valued. For example, the current price level of the S&P 500 index is too high for my taste. It is priced above its intrinsic value, and investing in it would seem to me to be a combination of low expected return and high risk. What about Berkshire stock? What is its intrinsic value?

Estimating the intrinsic value of Berkshire Hathaway stock is quite complex and tedious, much more so than for most conventional companies. On the other hand, it's also true that once an investor does manage to wade through it all, the reward for doing so will be greater than just to have an idea of what is the intrinsic value of the stock. An added advantage is that the effort involved in keeping this estimate up to date will be very small while its reliability will be above average. All of this is because Berkshire Hathaway's business is stable, slowly changing, and readily predictable.

Several methods can be used to estimate intrinsic value. Over time, we have tried estimating intrinsic value using four different methods. We found that their results differed so little that we ended up sticking with the most straightforward of these. This is based upon estimating the value of the two halves of the conglomerate separately and then adding the two values together. We start with the part of Berkshire that is invested in publicly traded stocks. Here, we make a few minor adjustments. If the stock portfolio seems too expensive, we can trim back its value. We make no such adjustments upward. In the cases of some items the accounting for which does not reflect market value, we adjust these to market value. For example, we do this with the investments in Kraft Heinz and Occidental Petroleum. At a time when interest rates were at zero, we slightly increased the value of cash. At current interest rates, we're not doing that. Adjusted in this manner, the portfolio value per share is approximately $426,000 in September 2024.

We then proceed to value the other part of the conglomerate, which consists of private companies. Here, we take their pretax profits, subtract the investment income of the insurance companies to avoid duplication, and multiply the total adjusted pretax profits by 14.4. Why 14.4? We consider a P/E of 16× to be reasonable for the entire private portion of Berkshire. This is roughly the long-term average at which U.S. stocks trade, perhaps even a bit lower. Given the quality of Berkshire's businesses, this seems sufficiently conservative. A P/E of 16× for after-tax earnings corresponds to a P/E of 14.4× for pretax earnings. That difference is smaller than would be consistent with the normal U.S. tax rate, because, for various reasons related to its structure and business types, Berkshire indeed has a lower overall tax rate. We then convert the result back to a per-share basis and add that to the value of the publicly traded portfolio. The total intrinsic value of a Berkshire Hathaway share to us in September 2024 was $728,000. The shares are therefore undervalued by about 5%.

Figure 2.2 shows the development of Berkshire Hathaway's share value as we have calculated it continuously each quarter since 2011 while

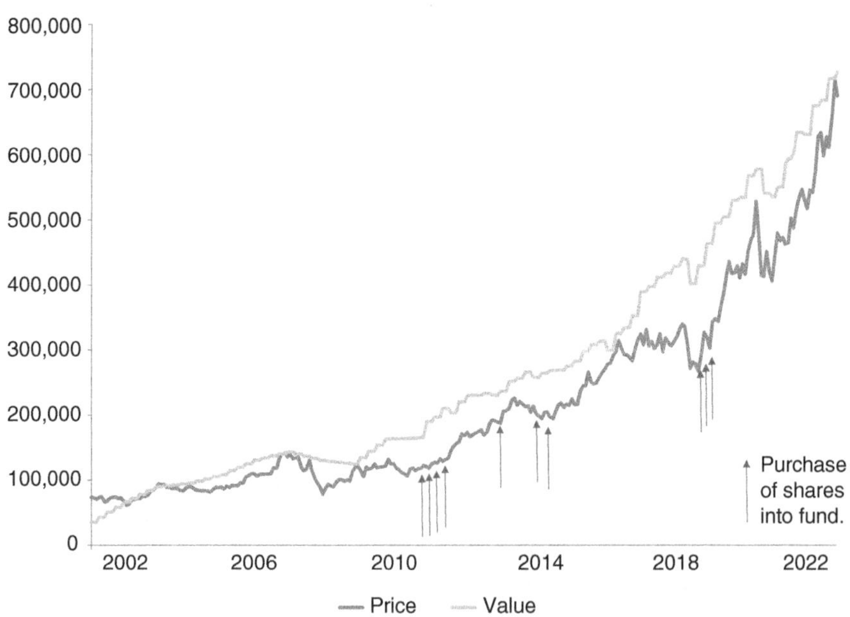

Figure 2.2 Development of Berkshire Hathaway's share price and value.
Source: Vltava Fund.

also calculating it back annually to 2000 and comparing it to the share price. The arrows show our buying moments.

We can make a couple of interesting observations from the chart. The intrinsic value is growing quite reliably, accelerating regularly and exponentially. This is logical because the company's invested capital is also growing exponentially. The share price in the long run follows the value development but with much greater volatility. This creates situations where the difference between price and value is greater than usual. These circumstances present attractive buying opportunities. The investor's returns, then, consist in the change in intrinsic value of the share and the change in the difference between price and value. This, in a nutshell, is the very description of value investing.

We expect similar development for many years into the future and with a relatively high probability. So why is the market overlooking this opportunity in the long term? There can never be a definitive answer to this question, but I believe it is a combination of several reasons. First, Berkshire is a company that is quite difficult to understand and analyze. A large proportion of investors will never get over this hurdle or even have the ability to do so. Second, this is not a business offering much hope of making a person quickly and fabulously rich. It does provide near certainty of high long-term returns, but who has such patience in today's markets? Moreover, investors in general tend to underestimate the long-term effects of compound interest, and that's precisely what Berkshire Hathaway is all about.

One can only wish that nothing will change in the approach that most investors take to Berkshire's stock. The ideal situation for us as long-term shareholders is for the share price to remain below its intrinsic value. This allows the company to buy back its own shares cheaply. Over the time we have held the stock, Berkshire has bought back and retired about 15% of its own shares. With each share that is bought back at a price below its intrinsic value, the intrinsic value of the remaining shares increases.

Berkshire's Future

Berkshire stock holds a very important position in Vltava Fund's portfolio. This is our oldest and, through most of the holding period, our largest position. We consider the shares to be a sort of cornerstone of our portfolio.

It is a stock from which we anticipate returns approximating 10% per annum over the long term, which is more than we expect from the equity markets generally. Moreover, it is a company with much less business risk than other companies. It therefore combines above-average return with below-average risk. When we are evaluating any other investment and considering whether to include it into the fund's portfolio, Berkshire stock is always a good benchmark. Every other stock bears greater risk, and it is therefore reasonable that we require that to be balanced by a higher return. Indeed, we can always add more Berkshire shares. It is likely that Berkshire shares will retain this position in our portfolio and in our high regard for still a long time to come.

Before we move on from Berkshire Hathaway, I still should touch upon the question of succession. Warren Buffett was born in 1930, and it is clear that his tenure at the company's helm is coming to an end. This is not pleasant to contemplate, but investors should not shy away from reality. So, what will Berkshire Hathaway look like after Buffett? It will be led by Greg Abel. He has already assumed much of his future responsibilities and the transition should be very smooth. The longer I follow him, the more I like him. Mainly because of his management experience, he may in some ways be even better than Warren Buffett. Todd Combs and Ted Weschler will have more of the public portfolio in their hands, and Ajit Jain will continue to run the insurance groups. Howard Buffett, Warren's son, will become chairman of the board. His main role will be to ensure that the company's entrepreneurial culture continues.

It has long been anticipated that Berkshire Hathaway's shareholder structure would change significantly over the years. Warren Buffett now owns about 15% of Berkshire's shares and controls about 30% of the voting rights. It had been intended that after his death his shares would go to charity organizations, which were to sell off the shares within a limited time and use the money. Thereby, Berkshire's now largest shareholder would have disappeared from the list of shareholders. In the summer of 2024, however, Buffett announced a change in his will. Upon his death, all his shares will pass to a foundation to be administered by his children. They would use 5% of the remaining Berkshire shares each year for charitable purposes. This means that Buffett's stock will represent an important share in the voting rights for longer than expected. The transformation to the post-Buffett era should therefore be more gradual.

In any case, Berkshire Hathaway will be in good hands. Its days of greatest growth in absolute numbers are still ahead of it. Whereas the fates of most companies and their life cycles are linked to the significance, importance, and life cycles of their products and services, Berkshire Hathaway is not dependent on one or a few products. In fact, it is in the business of compounding interest, and it can run onward and successfully for a long time to come.

Let me close with a bit of levity. In December 2016, when Berkshire stock was priced at about $240,000, I was playing around with the numbers and trying to guess when the share price would reach $1 million. My two starting assumptions were the expected growth in the company's value and the stock price that would equal its value at that point. I worked out that Berkshire's share price would reach that milestone on November 15, 2031. Yes, exactly November 15. Today, working with the same starting conditions, my estimate has already moved back to March 2029. These long-term forecasts are not to be taken too seriously, of course, but, in this case, they show that Berkshire's value has grown faster over these 8 years than we had expected. When the stock price does reach $1 million, I'll make a private guess for a price of $3 million and be curious to see by how much I miss it.

If I ever were to write my memoirs, they would be entitled *My Life in Numbers*. Investing is an ideal activity for someone who likes numbers. This can be a lot of fun. At Vltava Fund, we keep a lot of internal statistics. Some of them turn out to be useless or at least not very informative, but others have proven very useful. We have created various internal statistical models, and some of the autocorrelation models in particular provide a very quick picture as to the state of affairs. Paradoxically, however, we do not use any complex models when selecting and analyzing the individual stocks themselves. In fact, we regard these models as dangerous, because they easily can lead one to become blinded by apparent precision. Experience leads us in the opposite direction. An investment thesis must be so simple and obvious that all the calculations needed to formulate it can be done in your head.

Chapter 3

Asbury Automotive Group

Seeking Treasure Among Cannibals

A share cannibal is a company that hungrily buys back its own stock. In a figurative sense, the firm seems to be devouring itself. From the investment perspective of the existing stockholders, however, with each share that is cannibalized, their own stakes in the company grow without them having to do anything. There are many such companies in the markets. Among those that have seen their share numbers outstanding diminish rapidly due to buybacks include, for example, Ameriprice Financial, Applied Materials, Atkore, AutoNation, Dillards, Discover Financial Services, Dollarama, Domino's Pizza, NVR, O'Reilly Automotive, Pulte Group, Visa, and Williams-Sonoma. These companies have reduced their share counts by 30%, 40%, or even more than 70% over the past 15 years. They belong to a voracious tribe of cannibals, and because they have mostly been able to buy their own shares at good prices, the intrinsic value of the remaining shares has been rising nicely over the long term. You can see for yourself how this is reflected in their share prices.

A large part of Vltava Fund's portfolio today consists of stocks of companies that have been buying back their own shares at nontrivial pace over the long term and at prices that in our estimation are below their intrinsic values. This transfers some of the value from the selling shareholders to those who remain invested in the company. Analogously, if share buybacks are made at prices above their intrinsic value, then value is transferred in the opposite direction – from the shareholders who remain invested in the company to those shareholders who sell. As always, price matters.

Significant Changes to Our Fund's Portfolio

We consider well-executed share buybacks to be a major source of companies' value creation and we place great importance upon it in selecting our investments. This was not entirely the case in the past. For us, a change came at the beginning of 2020. This is associated with the upsurge in passive investing that I described in the introduction to the book. Passive investing is not a new phenomenon. It has been going on for some time and has also been gradually changing the nature and behavior of the markets over time. Already during the second decade of this century, we had observed that there were numerous companies doing very well in their businesses but that investors weren't really paying them much attention. Consequently, while their share prices were getting cheaper and cheaper, the money flows in the markets, increasingly influenced by passive investing, were almost completely passing them by. So, on the one hand, there were more and more attractive investment opportunities, but, on the other hand, the market was not taking notice. The price-discovery process was discernibly falling behind. We were contemplating how to react to this situation and how to try even to turn it to our advantage. Then the solution presented itself. If we were to put together a portfolio of growth companies whose shares were cheap and which at the same time were buying up their own shares on an ongoing basis and in large amounts, then we would not have to wait and rely on the market to notice their attractiveness and generate demand, because the companies were themselves creating demand for their shares through buybacks. The shares' low cost would then become a tangible advantage, and it would even be logical to wish that the market would ignore them for as long as possible. After all, the longer these shares would remain inexpensive, the more stock the companies would themselves be able to buy back cheaply and the greater the positive impact on the growth of their intrinsic value over time.

For us, the decisive impetus for this change came at the end of 2018, when equity markets were falling quite sharply and deeply and when their growing price inelasticity was perhaps more apparent than before. We decided to reanalyze hundreds of companies with share buybacks in mind. Although we had taken buybacks into account before, now we were going to view them with much greater importance. After about a year of work, we were ready to include these companies into the portfolio. Finding these companies is just a matter of doing a lot of work, but getting them into the portfolio is not a short-term matter. In fact, most of them are too expensive for our taste most of the time, and so we expected the buying to take a long time. Fate worked in our favor, however, because at almost the same time the world was hit by COVID-19, stocks plummeted briefly, but, above all, volatility increased for an extended period due to the new great uncertainty. High volatility is beneficial for investors in the sense that it brings good investment opportunities more often. When individual share prices fluctuate a lot, they often reach levels that enable investment.

Coincidentally, we know to the hour exactly when we started this targeted shift in portfolio composition. It was when the markets opened on March 24, 2020. At that time, stocks of companies for which share buybacks are a long-term and significant aspect of the asset allocation made up 38% of our portfolio. Today, it's almost 90%, and this strategy is delivering very good returns. One of the companies in Vltava Fund's portfolio that belongs to this group and whose shares have been added to the portfolio since 2020 is Asbury Automotive Group (ABG). This is another share cannibal. Over the past 15 years, the number of ABG shares outstanding has fallen by a third. This means that any shareholder who bought ABG shares 15 years ago has seen their ownership position in the company increase by half in that time — without having to buy another share. Moreover, the company itself has experienced dramatic growth in the intervening years.

ABG

Asbury Automotive Group, Inc., is one of the largest franchised automobile dealerships in the United States, with 157 new-vehicle dealerships in 15 states. There are several publicly traded companies in the United States in this business. In addition to ABG, some of the larger ones include AutoNation, Lithia Motors, and Penske Automotive Group. It's also worth noting that Berkshire Hathaway owns one of the leading car dealership groups. Berkshire bought the Van Huyl Group in 2015. Today it has been renamed Berkshire Hathaway Automotive and has more than 100 dealerships.

The entire industry is highly fragmented. I estimate that there are approximately 17,000 car dealerships in the United States. The biggest player in the market is AutoNation with just over 300 stores. Its market share, if we count it by number of outlets, is therefore just under 2%. ABG's market share is around 1%. The industry has been gradually consolidating over the long term. The number of selling points today is only about half that of the 1960s and about a quarter less than in the 1980s. Consolidation can be expected to continue, as market conditions and market structure favor larger players rather than family-owned companies or entities with few retail outlets. Part of the investment rationale for ABG is based on the continued consolidation of the sector, from which ABG should expect further significant benefits.

ABG's business is itself typical of most dealers in the auto market. It can be divided into four parts: new car sales, used car sales, service and spare parts, and financing and insurance. See Figure 3.1.

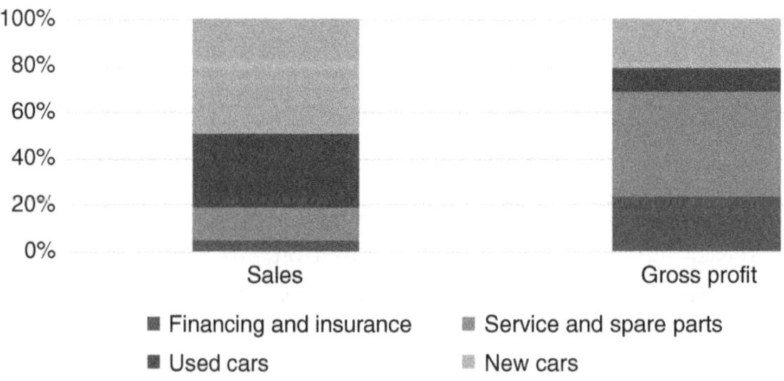

Figure 3.1   Asbury Group: revenue and profit structure.
Source: Asbury Group.

Figure 3.1 shows that all four parts of ABG's business contribute to sales and profit differently. While new cars account for almost half of sales, and while new and used cars together account for 81%, their combined contribution to profit is only 31%. Service and spare parts, together with financing and insurance, account for the majority of profits. The whole business is therefore less cyclical than would appear at first sight. The greater cyclicality in car sales is offset by the more modest cyclicality in service and spare parts. These are largely a function of miles driven and car age.

Each of these four parts of ABG's business also has quite different profit margins. Just to give you an idea, the average price of a new car at ABG is around $50,000, and the gross profit per car is around $3,500. The average price of a used car is around $30,000, and the gross profit per car is around $1,500. This represents gross margins of 7% and 5%. Service and spare parts have a gross margin of around 50% and financing and insurance almost 100%. The latter is a brokerage commission, because ABG does not provide its own insurance and financing to customers. One could almost say that new car sales serve as a way to win customers, knowing that the main profit from the customer relationship will be generated by other services and over time: first by arranging insurance and financing, then by providing service and spare parts throughout ownership of the car, and finally by selling the used car.

ABG sells cars of almost all brands. The luxury segment accounts for 30% of sales and includes such brands as Lexus, Mercedes-Benz, BMW, and Porsche. That 30% is more than the luxury segment's share in the market overall, which is positive for ABG because customers who buy luxury cars are less price sensitive and their behavior is less cyclical. Of the remainder, imported cars (Toyota, Honda, Hyundai, etc.) make up 40% and domestically produced cars (Ford, Stellantis, GM) contribute 30%. In 2020, ABG introduced a new service called Clicklane that allows customers to buy cars purely online. The first years of experience with Clicklane indicate great added value in this form of sales, because about 90% of the customers who buy a car this way are new to ABG and become a source of additional revenue if they use ABG's services during the ownership period.

ABG's long-term financial performance is excellent. Over the past 10 years, from 2013 to 2023, revenue has grown from $5.3 billion to $14.8 billion (by 1.8×), net income from $101 million to $683 million (by 5.7×), and earnings per share from $3.25 to $32.60 (by 9×). Earnings per share are growing much faster than earnings alone, because the number of shares outstanding has been reduced from 30.7 million to 20 million in 10 years' time through share buybacks. ABG is one hungry share cannibal.

ABG's rapid growth is founded on very efficient capital allocation supported by high operating efficiency. The company generates abundant free cash flow even after capital expenditures. The cash is essentially channeled in one of three main directions: to acquisitions, share buybacks, or debt repayments. Historically, the largest amount of cash has gone into acquisitions. Just in recent years, ABG has brought in nearly $10 billion in new revenue through acquisitions, and the size of individual acquisitions has tended to increase as the company itself grows. ABG's management has been patient, however, and in periods when it has not been presented with opportunities for further acquisitions to suit its vision, it has directed capital largely into share buybacks and debt repayments, thereby bolstering its financial capacity for further acquisitions in the future. The number of shares has fallen by more than one-third in the past decade, while debt remains within a range that management has set for itself as optimal.

ABG still has a lot of potential for more growth, especially through acquisitions. The fragmented car dealers market still offers ample scope for this, and ABG's management regards growth by acquisitions as an important part of its long-term strategy. It is realistic to expect that by the end of this decade ABG could again double in size as measured by sales. The positive impact on earnings per share from this doubling will be further bolstered by the continuing reduction in shares outstanding as a result of ongoing share buybacks.

If I were to sum it all up, ABG is a company that is growing fast in its absolute size but faster still on a per-share basis. One would expect its stock to trade at higher than single-digit earnings multiples, and yet the opposite is true. ABG's stock can routinely be bought at P/Es well below 10×. Why is the market blind to this opportunity? ABG is a company with a market capitalization of less than $5 billion. That's too small to be included in the major market indices. The official sector breakdown places it into the consumer cyclical goods sector and into the auto and truck sales segment. When investors hear words like "cyclical" and "cars," they usually would rather look elsewhere. We now have ABG in Vltava Fund's portfolio, and a few years earlier we had had shares of AutoNation, its competitor and another voracious share cannibal. In all the time we have been following this sector and actively investing in it, we have been able to observe how most investors undervalue these companies or even tend to ignore them altogether.

For investors looking for value in stocks, this is an ideal situation. If a value investor is a long-term owner of ABG stock, then their main wish should be that the market continues to ignore the stock for as long as possible. We consider ABG to be a hidden investment treasure and hope it remains little noticed well into the future. Indeed, if the stock stays out of the main interest of investors, thereby allowing the company to buy its own shares in large volumes at six, seven, or eight times earnings, then value creation on a per-share basis will continue very rapidly and with dramatic positive impact on the share price. As they say, "Ignorance is bliss."

The Importance of Capital Allocation

Before we move on to the next company, let me make a couple more general comments on the subject of share buybacks. Company management has a wide range of possibilities in allocating capital. They can invest it back into their own businesses in the form of capital spending (for either maintenance or growth), into research and development, or into selling, general, and administration expenses. In a growing business, some of the additional capital will typically be swallowed up by strengthening working capital. Another relatively common direction in which capital flows is to acquisitions. If all attractive possibilities as mentioned are exhausted, the capital can be used to reduce debt or it can be paid out to shareholders. There are essentially two basic options for paying out capital to shareholders: by paying dividends or through buying back the company's own shares.

Some of the possibilities mentioned also may occur in reverse. Not only can the company buy back its own shares, but it also can issue new shares. Debt can be reduced but also increased, and the opposite of acquisitions would be to sell some assets. The main source of capital for companies in the long term tends to be their own generated profit. Debt comes second. Speaking generally, it can be said that companies growing at rates faster than their return on invested capital (ROIC) likely need to raise external capital, and companies growing slower than their ROIC tend to have excess capital and are more concerned with where to allocate it.

So, every CEO has several options for generating capital on the one hand and even more possibilities for allocating capital on the other. Theoretically, a CEO should always consider all the options available on both sides of the scales, compare the profitability of each capital allocation variant (while taking into account the associated risks), and then choose those possibilities promising the highest returns. From our investor's perspective, good and well-managed companies can be considered those that have high overall return on invested capital (ROIC). Corporate management can then be considered an efficient asset allocator if there is a high return on incremental invested capital (ROIIC).

Now let's consider those types of asset allocation that channel capital from companies to shareholders. This occurs in fundamentally three ways: by paying dividends, by buying back the company's own shares, or by selling the whole company. Selling the whole company is a bit of a special case, so we will put it aside and focus upon dividends and share buybacks. These are important items in companies' overall capital allocation, can have big impacts on a company's value, and often are rather misunderstood by shareholders. Dividends are historically older and in earlier times constituted the preferred form of paying out money to shareholders. In recent decades, however, share buybacks have become increasingly prominent, and in the U.S. market, for example, they now surpass dividends in importance.

Many investors buy certain stocks because of their dividends. They like to have the dividend money landing in their accounts on a regular basis. This more or less regular and predictable income gives them the feeling that they are actually getting something from the companies they own. That may be true, but the reality is that dividend payments alone do not make an investor richer. This is just an illusion, which can be thought of as a standard psychological error in reasoning known as *mental accounting*. In mental accounting, investors evaluate dividends separately and apart from the rest of their investments, which is a mistake. Although dividend payments do represent a nice cash flow for the investor, they come at the expense of the "principal" or value further held by means of the shares.

Receiving a payment from a dividend does not really create wealth. This can be easily demonstrated in simple numbers. Imagine that shareholders collectively own a company that has equity of $1 billion before dividends are paid. When the company pays a dividend of $50 million to the shareholders, the shareholders then own a stake in a company with equity of $950 million plus they have $50 million in cash. Their wealth is unchanged by the dividend payment. In essence, it can be said that they have been paid something that they had already owned through shares. The same conclusion is reached by standard valuation models, which set the value of a company as the sum of discounted future cash flows minus net debt. The payment of dividends increases the company's net debt and reduces its value accordingly by exactly the amount received by shareholders in dividends. After all, the stock market quotation reflects this, too, as dividend stocks tend to open on an ex-dividend date (which is the first day that a stock trades without a dividend declared earlier) at a price one dividend payment lower than where the stock had closed the day before. In the real world, where taxes are paid on dividends, the shareholders are worse off after dividend payments by the amount of the dividend withholding tax. Financial theory speaks of the so-called dividend fallacy. The *dividend fallacy* – a belief that dividends are "free money" – is one of the most common mistakes investors make. In reality, dividends are not "free money," and this simple and trivial matter is sometimes almost impossible to explain to some people.

The dividend policies of companies must be considered, therefore, in the context of their overall asset allocations. Dividends are beneficial if a company has surplus capital, does not have too much debt, and has no better use for that capital. In practice, unfortunately, it is often the case that when considering capital allocation, corporate management prefers to cut off a portion for dividends without giving much thought to whether this is the best use of resources. Dividend policy is often established in advance and quite rigidly. Most common dividend plans assume a regularly increasing dividend, a minimum "guaranteed" dividend, or a fixed payout ratio (calculated as dividend/earnings). Management does this knowing that investors (and stock analysts) like things to be regular and predictable and while understanding full well that dividends often have a special status in the eyes of investors due to their mental accounting. Moreover, they fear that investors would interpret a dividend cut or even its elimination as an admission of concern for the company's future. This does not, however, make much sense from the viewpoint of the companies themselves and their capital allocation. If management has an attractive opportunity through which to invest capital, it should assign to that opportunity maximum priority and simply not pay any dividend. Conversely, in cases where the business does not have attractive investment opportunities, it would make sense to pay an unusually large dividend. This manner of thinking is entirely normal in the world of privately held companies, but it is altogether rare in that of publicly traded ones. We have companies in our portfolio for which we think their paying relatively high dividends is the right thing to do (e.g., S&U, Quálitas Controladora) as well as companies for which we are happy they do not pay dividends and would even consider their doing so to be a mistake (e.g., Berkshire Hathaway, Markel).

Now, what about share buybacks? Do they bring value to shareholders? The answer depends upon the price at which those shares are bought in. If a company buys back its own shares at a price equal to the actual value of those shares, then 100 cents are exchanged for $1 (or €1) and no value is created. The only change is that some shareholders retained their shares in the company and others exchanged them for cash. What happens if the company buys back its own shares at a price lower than the actual value of those shares? In these buybacks, those shareholders who sell receive less for their stock than the shares are really worth, and the value of the shares still held by the other shareholders increases along with those shareholders' percentage ownership of the company. That means there is a transfer of wealth from the selling shareholders to those who still hold the shares. Analogously, if share buybacks occur at a price higher than the real value of the shares, then wealth is transferred from the shareholders retaining their shares to those who sold. So, the price at which share buybacks are made matters a great deal in evaluating those buybacks. Last year, companies in the U.S. market spent approximately $1 trillion on share buybacks. In our view, the majority of those buybacks were made at prices above the value of the shares and were therefore capital-destroying from the continuing shareholders' point of view. Often, companies buy back their shares to immunize (cover) the impact of massive share issues to management and employees (so-called stock-based compensation, or SBC).

We often regard share buybacks made at prices below the value of the shares to be the best use of capital. This is essentially an investment by the company into itself with a return on capital usually higher than is offered by available investment opportunities and without the risk associated with large acquisitions. If management can maintain the discipline to buy back shares only at favorable prices, and if this is not at the cost of excessively growing the debt, then share buybacks can have a highly positive impact on both share value and share price over the long term. The current shape and structure of stock markets offers a whole range of such shares due to the prevalence of passive investing.

Chapter 4

Alimentation Couche-Tard

Seeking Treasure Among Acquisition Masters

For many companies, buying back their own shares is indeed the best use of capital, the best investment, and the best choice from the shareholders' viewpoint. Often, however, companies prefer other and demonstrably inferior ways to allocate capital. Many times, this is because the CEO of the company desires to enter the history books with renown for concluding a glorious transaction. Now, I understand that the phrase "bought two of its largest competitors" sounds much more grandiose on a résumé than does "bought back one-fifth of the company's own shares," but this kind of thinking comes with big risk for shareholders. Acquisitions invariably look good on paper and in management's projections. The reality, however, is often quite different.

Our study of market events and our own investment experience lead us to conclude that the greatest potential risk for value destruction in asset allocation is through acquisitions. This is because, overall, it is a form of capital allocation to which the largest volumes of money are directed. In individual cases, the sums can be enormous compared to the size and capitalization of the acquiring company. Moreover, in these transactions, management's egos may play a large role, and their interests and objectives most often diverge from those of shareholders. Furthermore, management's appetite for acquisitions has a cyclical character. It increases as share prices rise, and the greatest number of acquisitions generally occur when a bull market is near its peak. The room for error is simply greatest here. We consider the worst acquisitions to be those that are very large, that are paid for with stock instead of cash, and that are outside the buyer's existing core business area. It often is the case, too, that the announcement of these acquisitions is unexpected, the market is caught off guard by it, and there follows an immediate negative price reaction. Our portfolio has itself seen two instances of these large acquisitions in recent years, when Sanofi acquired Genzyme in 2011 and Teva bought Allergan in 2015. In both cases, our decision quickly to sell these stocks proved to be correct. Another such case will be discussed in Chapter 17. We try to avoid companies and management that have a history of making large acquisitions or where there is a risk of their making them.

Nevertheless, it should also be said that there are some companies that for a long time have based their growth upon acquisitions and have done well. They do not overpay for individual acquisitions, they are able to integrate them well, they do not have megalomaniacal plans, and when there are no attractive acquisitions available, they can wait patiently for the next opportunity. In such companies, then, acquisitions do not destroy value but create it. An example of such a company in our portfolio is Alimentation Couche-Tard. It is no coincidence that this company remains controlled by its founders, who to this day still own a substantial stake in it and therefore think about these things as do real shareholders.

The Winking Owl

Alimentation Couche-Tard (ATD) is one of Canada's most interesting and successful business stories. Contributing especially to that story is its founder, Alain Bouchard. Bouchard is a born Québécois and at the start of his career spent a 12-year apprenticeship in various positions with several retail companies in his native Canada. In 1980, at the age of 31, he decided to set up his own business and opened his first convenience store in Laval. He came up with a groundbreaking idea for its time, which was to keep the store open 24 hours a day. Corresponding well to this concept are the winking owl of its logo and the name of the company (the *Couche-Tard* translating loosely as "night owl"). The company grew successfully, slowly at first, then faster and faster both organically and through larger and larger acquisitions. Today, ATD has nearly 17,000 stores in Canada, the United States, Northern Europe, and Asia. Most of these also have gas stations. With sales of more than $70 billion a year, it is one of the largest global companies in its industry. ATD's main brand, Circle K, can be seen and visited quite often when one travels in North America or the more northern regions of Europe. Whenever I pass one, I never fail to stop and go inside to take a look around and get a firsthand impression as a customer.

To grow gradually from one store and miniscule sales to 17,000 stores and sales exceeding $70 billion takes time, clear vision, and a huge measure of management skill. Acquisitions have provided the main source of growth through the company's 40+ years in existence. Of all the stores ATD operates today, 75% came through acquisitions. Few companies have been able to grow successfully over the long term through acquisitions. ATD is among the most successful of these. The company chooses its acquisitions well to ensure not only financial but also strategic benefits. It does not pay exorbitant prices, and the acquired companies generally perform better in ATD's hands than when they were still standing on their own. In periods between individual acquisitions, ATD reduces its debt quickly. Indebtedness is maintained over the long term at a level that almost always allows management both to buy back the company's own shares and to have financial capacity to spare for further potential acquisitions.

In the 44 years since its founding, ATD has made several dozen acquisitions. We are not aware of any that could be regarded as detrimental. This is reflected in, among other aspects, ATD's return on invested capital, which has been not only high over the long term but also relatively stable, with no visible jumps affected by acquisitions. ATD's beginnings were modest. From the time the first store opened in 1980, it took 5 years to grow the network to 34 stores and another 9 years to grow to 304 stores in 1995. Individual acquisitions have gradually increased, and as ATD and its capital have grown, so, too, have the size of those acquisitions.

Acquisitions in 2004, 2014, 2015, 2018, and 2023 each expanded the number of stores by more than 1,000. Over the past 20 years, ATD has made a total of 75 acquisitions, bringing with them about 13,000 stores. Today, it operates more than 17,000 stores in 25 countries. ATD's main markets are its home market of Canada, the United States, and North and Northwest Europe. The scope for further significant growth remains enormous and ATD has clear ambitions to pursue it. In the United States alone, ATD's largest market, there now exist an estimated 150,000 convenience stores and gas stations of the type ATD operates. Among these, about 90,000 are stand-alone stores and 60,000 belong to chains. ATD itself has around 7,000 stores in the United States today. This is less than 5% of the total market. Similarly large potential for growth can be seen in other parts of the world, including in Europe, where the last big acquisition was made; in Asia, where ATD is still rather small; and in Latin America, where ATD scarcely has any presence so far. Acquisitions should play a key role in future growth. Not long before this book went to press, ATD had announced that it was negotiating to buy one of its biggest competitors, Japan's Seven & i Holdings Co., Ltd. It seems that the night owl never sleeps.

As in many other industries, in the case of convenience stores, and especially of gas stations, the gradually changing structure of the industry and its expense structure favors the big players over the small ones. ATD is, among other things, one of the world's largest buyers of fuels. This is a business segment wherein economies of scale are substantial and gradual consolidation – with more market share going to the big chains – is expected to continue. ATD has the financial strength and management skills to succeed in this competitive environment.

When Are Acquisitions Beneficial?

Stock investing is based on a simple idea. A company invests a certain amount of capital into its business. This grows over time through the company's activities, the increments are reinvested into the business, the amount of invested capital increases, and the returns grow in absolute terms along with the capital. These are reinvested again, and so on and so forth. From an investment point of view, the most attractive companies are those that achieve high returns on capital and are able to reinvest that capital repeatedly with equally high returns.

Historically, the largest part of companies' capital (approximately one-fifth) goes to mergers and acquisitions. (Other large items in capital allocation are selling, general, and administrative [SG&A] expenses; capital expenditures; share repurchases; and dividends). Unfortunately, acquisitions destroy value in many cases. But if management can do acquisitions well, they can be a source of great competitive advantage and a powerful driver of growth.

How can one measure management's success when it comes to acquisitions? Surely it is not enough just that a company grows as a result of acquisitions. A CEO whose company retains a profit equal to 10% of net worth each year is responsible after 10 years in the role for deploying more than 60% of all the capital in the company. Such growth is, of course, likely to be accompanied by an increase in profitability, but that does not in itself mean that management is doing a good job and allocating capital efficiently.

The benchmark for evaluating management needs to be much more rigorous than that. We will be interested in what returns the new, additional invested capital brings. Two formulas are used for this purpose. The first calculates the return on invested capital (ROIC). This is our starting point and shows how efficiently the company's existing capital is being used.

$$ROIC = \frac{Net\ profit}{Invested\ capital}$$

$$ROIIC = \frac{Net\ profit_1 - Net\ profit_0}{Invested\ capital_1 - Invested\ capital_0}$$

The second formula calculates the return on incremental invested capital (ROIIC). It shows how the company's profitability increased due to the incremental capital invested. Company management often defend their planned acquisitions with arguments such as that they will increase profits, that they will bring the required return on capital from the third year onwards, and so forth. Typical phrases we hear in these cases are, for example, "earnings accretive in year 2," "earning the hurdle rate of capital in year 4," and "significant synergies." But those criteria are too soft. If a large sum of money is taken for an acquisition and it brings new, additional business to the company, then it is usually logical that profits will increase as well. The relevant question, however, is whether the increase in profit is sufficient relative to the additional capital invested in the business after the acquisition. If the return on the additional capital invested is high and at least exceeds the company's cost of capital, then the acquisition can be said to add value for shareholders. But even this should not be a sufficient criterion for evaluating an acquisition. Ideally, the assessment should examine whether the return on the additional capital invested in the form of an acquisition exceeds the likely returns from all other options available and to which that capital could also have been allocated. This is where corporate management often fails, as well as where investors and analysts often fail when assessing the merits of an acquisition.

The paramount mission of a company's management (often forgotten) should be to maximize the value of the company per issued share. Capital allocation plays a key role in this. For market participants who measure the time of their shareholding in days or weeks, these considerations are irrelevant. For investors like us, however, who view shares primarily as a stake in a company's business enterprise and the point of investing in shares as the long-term effect of values created by humans and compounded returns on capital, these considerations are crucial. When we analyze some company as a potential investment, we consider it ideal for a CEO to have two fundamental skill sets: to be able to manage the company's business well and to be capable to allocate the earned capital efficiently. In practice, it is much more common that a CEO performs better as a business manager and poorer as an investor in allocating capital. This is altogether understandable, as a large part of company bosses have worked their way up to their positions during their time in the industry and primarily thanks to their professional and managerial capabilities. Once they reach the very top of the company, however, they are suddenly given an additional set of responsibilities related to capital allocation. This activity requires a completely different mindset, skills, and aptitudes, and its successful mastery is much rarer in practice. A CEO who can manage a business well and, moreover, allocate earned capital excellently, is a golden treasure, especially if their tenure is for the long term.

To be successful, a CEO must not only possess the right skills but also must think and act like a shareholder. Their goals and motivation matter a lot. Oftentimes, we find that such is not the case. This is a textbook example of what is termed the *agent-principal problem*. Its essence is that there often exists a conflict between the interests and priorities of managers, who are in the position of hired "agent," and the owners (shareholders), who are in the position of the "principals." Management is acting on behalf of an entity that is owned by somebody else. Management often has its own objectives. First and foremost, it is concerned with its own remuneration and the importance and prestige related to the size of the business it runs. Managers often prioritize their career risk and generally have a shorter thinking horizon. Corporate shareholders are not really interested in these things. They are (or should be) interested in long-term value creation per share they own. How closely management succeeds in aligning its own goals and ambitions with those of its shareholders is very often determined by the way it allocates assets.

It is often in acquisitions that the biggest capital allocation errors and the greatest value destruction occur. Management's ego plays an important role here. Acquisitions in general, meaning their size, frequency, and susceptibility to error, are strongly and positively correlated with developments in both the stock market and the economy. During my investment career, corporate acquisition activity has had peaks in 1999, 2007, 2015, and 2021 and lows in 1991, 2002, 2009, and 2020. The link to developments in stock markets is obvious here at first glance. Acquisitions peak when markets are high and slow down when markets are low.

When we evaluate a newly announced acquisition, there are some basic characteristics of the transaction that can suggest whether the acquisition will create or destroy shareholder value. Acquisitions where the buying company pays in cash tend to be better value creators than are acquisitions paid for with stock. Paying in stock often seduces management into thinking that it costs nothing, which obviously is not true. When paying in stock, one has to sacrifice a part of one's own company to acquire part of another company. It all very much depends upon the share prices and the exchange ratio at which the transaction occurs. Acquisitions also turn out better when the business being purchased is similar to the one operated by the acquiring company. Examples of such acquisitions include historical transactions of companies like ATD or Constellation Software. Contrast this with so-called "transformational" acquisitions, where the buying company embarks on something that is intended to completely or significantly change its own shape. A case in point is the notoriously infamous purchase of media company Time Warner by Internet service provider AOL.

The success of an acquiring company's acquisition history may also provide some guidance. This often tends to be better if the company has a dedicated acquisition team and if acquisitions have been a key part of its strategy for a long time. Such companies tend to be much better prepared for acquisitions than are companies where the CEO wakes up one day to find that the idea of a big acquisition has been born in the meanders of his mind. Last but not least, of course, is the price at which an acquisition takes place. Michael Mauboussin and Dan Callahan, in their 2023 article "Total Shareholder Return," report that the average premium over market price for acquisitions between 1985 and 2021 was 45%. For large transactions, it was 30%. Acquisitions very often damage and reduce the value of the buying companies and, paradoxically, tend to be more advantageous for shareholders of the company being bought. In the hands of skillful and capable management, however, acquisitions can be a great tool for creating shareholder value. Indeed, they allow one to make what is, from a long-term perspective, the most important argument for investing in stocks: reinvest the capital earned over and over again so that there is rapid accumulation of its size and returns. ATD management's historical track record demonstrates that ATD is a company that knows how to make acquisitions, has derived significant long-term benefit from them, and is likely to continue to gain greatly from them in the future. ATD's return on capital and its rate of capital accumulation are significantly greater than those of the stock market overall and, therefore, ATD's stock returns can be expected to continue to outperform the market over the long term. ATD stock has held a solid place in Vltava Fund's portfolio since 2017, and we believe that, in absolute numbers, ATD's greatest growth is yet to come.

Chapter 5

Burford Capital

Seeking Treasure in People

In the expanded edition of my book *Equity Investing*, I introduced the Wealth Creation Formula. It looks like this:

$$\text{Wealth} = \left(\text{Human Factor} + \text{Risk}\right) \times \text{Capital Accumulation}$$

What I wanted to convey simply in constructing this formula was that if an investor wants their wealth to grow rapidly over the long term, they must base their portfolio on investments where the influence of the human factor on their value is high and where capital accumulates at a rapid rate over the long term. Let's think a little deeper about the concept of the human factor. I see every company as a living organism where people work to create value through their ideas, efforts, creativity, and everyday work. It doesn't always have to be successful, but, on average and over the long term, this influence is highly positive, and, above all, it is not eroded by the diminishing value of money. Everyone will probably acknowledge, for example, that Jeff Bezos' influence on the value of Amazon has been enormous. Similarly, the influence of Steve Jobs on the value of Apple or that of Warren Buffett on the value of Berkshire Hathaway, for instance, has been huge. People are simply the main drivers of value in a firm, at all levels. By no means does this apply only to giant corporations. People also create value on a smaller scale, for example in small businesses, services, and commerce. All of us either know these stories from our own environments or are directly striving to do this ourselves in our own firms.

The impact of human activity on the value of a company is altogether fundamental. People cannot influence the value of other asset classes (cash, gold, bonds) through their work, or they are limited by the opportunities the asset gives them to do so (land, real estate). Companies offer the greatest scope, flexibility, and possibilities for adapting to changing conditions. This is the first and foremost reason why owning equities does and must yield higher returns over the long term than would owning other major asset classes. That's not going to change in the future. Now, so far as individual companies are concerned, the influence of the human factor is not always of the same magnitude. It tends to be greater for companies in the services sector. Companies for which the human factor is very strong include, for example, Burford Capital. In principle, Burford can be equated with human capital.

The Young Litigation Finance Sector

A few years back, I was going through all the companies whose shares trade on the London Stock Exchange's Alternative Investment Market (AIM), and among them I found one name that I hadn't heard before: Burford Capital. It had litigation finance in its business description, which was also something new to me at the time. I was intrigued and decided to study Burford in more detail. I found it to be one of the most extraordinary companies with which I had come into contact in years. It was literally a hidden investment treasure. That was sometime in 2019. Our interest in Burford grew even more thanks to a lucky coincidence. In the summer of 2019, Muddy Waters came out with a very critical analytical report on Burford. Today, several years later, it is possible to say unequivocally that

Muddy Waters was mistaken on virtually every point. Nevertheless, publication of the report brought very negative publicity to Burford's shares, and their price fell for some time by about three-quarters: from around £15 to below £4. Thanks to this confluence of circumstances, at one point we were looking at shares in a company whose business and performance we admired and a share price that was extremely attractive. We bought Burford shares for the Vltava Fund portfolio.

Burford Capital is based in the United Kingdom but has a global reach and operates in a young sector known as *litigation finance*. It was founded in 2009 by two lawyers, Christopher Bogart and Jonathan Molot. Burford is a global leader and pioneer in its sector and is helping to shape that sector through its work.

The term *litigation finance* is not yet widely known, although it already has acquired the portmanteau name *litfin*. To put this into common language, this means that Burford helps various large corporations, law firms, individuals, and possibly other entities to finance their litigations in exchange for a share of any potential compensation awarded by a court. Of course, Burford also bears the full risk of failure. It is difficult to imagine a business enterprise where the outcome would depend more on the skills, knowledge, and experience of the people doing the job. Being able to assess a court case purely from a lawyer's perspective is one thing. It is also necessary, however, to know how to work with probabilities and time horizons and be able to express all this in monetary terms.

The market for litigation finance activity is huge and provides great potential for further growth of companies operating within it. Globally, annual legal fees are slowly climbing toward $1 trillion. Of this amount, more than half is attributable to the United States. The United States together with the United Kingdom, Australia, and Singapore are the most established markets for litfin services. Adoption within the EU is slightly behind. There are only a few dozen companies in the whole sector, and Burford is by far the largest of those that are publicly traded. Also in the business are several specialist litfin funds (Longford Capital Management, Parabellum Capital), some multistrategy funds (D. E. Shaw, Fortress), and a few insurance brokers. The barriers to entry into the industry may seem low, but the barriers to achieving massive scale and an ability to succeed over the long term stand quite high. One of Burford's competitive advantages is that it has more proprietary historical data related to the litigation it is involved in than do its competitors. Because litigation most often ends in a settlement agreement, which is generally confidential, data on the litigation process is available only to those parties directly involved. Thus, an outside observer wanting to estimate the probabilities associated with outcomes of new court cases is at a disadvantage. Compared to Burford, such observer has less data based upon which to form their own judgment.

Burford has a very broad clientele. The greater part is made up of large corporations and leading global law firms. Why do these large clients take advantage of the possibility to have their own litigation financed? Law firms generally are organized as partnerships, the vast majority of what they earn goes to pay employees, and they don't usually have a lot of equity that they can or are willing to invest into litigation. This is not just because litigation has an uncertain outcome but also because it can go on for many years and there is a mismatch in the timing between incoming cash flows and the remuneration of those who have worked on a case. This is why they turn to companies like Burford to finance their litigation. When Burford provides funding, it takes upon itself the financial risk of the law firm. If a lawsuit ends in defeat, the entire cost of funding it is Burford's loss. If the case ends in a win with a financial settlement, Burford typically first gets back the money it invested into the case and then shares the rest with the law firm according to a ratio agreed in advance. Burford usually does not take control of the litigation or initiate any litigation itself. It acts merely as a financial investor.

Motivations for large corporations to use Burford's services may be somewhat different from those of law firms. What both client groups have in common is that they will transfer the risk of loss to Burford in exchange for a lower share of the win. Corporations may have another reason that is related to accounting. This is because litigation expenses are a normal cost of the current year and reduce the corporation's profits. Litigation proceeds, on the other hand, are a one-time item, and investors tend not to take them into account. In utilizing the services of litigation finance companies, the CFO of a corporation can avoid the ongoing costs of litigation and instead can receive immediate cash that can be put to further use.

Dispute with Argentina Over $16 Billion

A third group of clients then consists of those who do not have the financial strength to pursue a long and costly litigation to claim damages.

This includes the most famous and by far the largest litigation that Burford is financing. It concerns the expropriation of shares in the Argentine oil company YPF. In 1993, YPF shares began trading on the New York Stock Exchange, and their listing there was part of a broader strategy to privatize Argentina's energy sector. Because Argentina has a rather wild history of state bankruptcies and respect for property rights, the Argentine state wrote directly into YPF's articles of association that shareholders must be compensated if ever YPF shares would happen to be expropriated. It even included a method for calculating that compensation. In so doing, the Argentine government was trying to reduce investors' fears and make them more willing to buy YPF shares. In 2012, the expropriation of YPF shareholders did indeed take place, but they did not receive compensation of any kind from Argentina. YPF's largest shareholder was the Spanish company Repsol. It agreed to a settlement of $5 billion with Argentina in 2014, apparently under pressure from and with the intervention of the Spanish government. The other major shareholder, Petersen Energía Inversora, which held 25% of the shares, got nothing, was forced to declare bankruptcy, and was left entirely penniless. The company's liquidator then approached Burford to finance a lawsuit against Argentina. In this exceptional case, Burford also took the lead in the case and brought in another former YPF shareholder, Eton Park Capital Management, to join Petersen Energía Inversora as a plaintiff.

The dispute with Argentina has been ongoing for a number of years. A very large sum of money is at stake, and Argentina is, of course, fighting tooth and nail in its defense. The lawsuits are playing out in the State of New York because that is where YPF shares were traded. All court judgments that have been handed down so far in this dispute have been in favor of the plaintiff (i.e., Burford and clients it represents). As of the end of summer 2023, an amount that Argentina should pay to the two shareholders represented by Burford as compensation for the earlier expropriation of YPF shares had already been determined. This is approximately $16 billion, which in monetary terms makes this one of the largest lawsuits of its kind in history. Moreover, the amount is not final because the sum continues to accrue interest until it will be paid. This amount is growing by more than $2 million a day and now exceeds $17 billion. Of the original $16 billion, the share attributable directly to Burford would be approximately $6 billion. That's a lot of money compared to Burford's market capitalization of less than $3 billion. It is therefore quite evident that the market does not believe Burford will be able to obtain the full amount. I share that view, and I expect that eventually there will be a settlement agreement between the two sides that will include a smaller amount and probably spread out over time. This nevertheless will likely still be a sum that is large compared to the size of Burford as a whole and may still exceed its current market capitalization. Currently, Argentina is running out of options to find its own path to victory through the courts. So far, the court has always ruled against it in this case. Argentina's appeal is currently pending before the Second Circuit Court of Appeals in New York, which is likely the court of final instance. In the meantime, the amount awarded to the party represented by Burford is recoverable, and the recovery process is already underway. It's going to get very interesting.

The Argentina litigation is the largest, but far from the only case in Burford's investment portfolio. Burford currently has approximately $5 billion invested in litigation, which it holds directly on its own balance sheet. Of this amount, and as valued today on an accounting basis, costs of the lawsuit with Argentina come to approximately $1.4 billion. In addition, Burford manages about another $2.3 billion of external assets that it coinvests into individual cases on an ongoing basis. In its financial statements and presentations, Burford provides a wealth of data depicting the company's value and potential. Over the course of its existence, since 2009, Burford has invested $1.5 billion in lawsuits that have been completed and settled. It has recovered more than $2.9 billion. This means that the total return on invested capital (ROIC) from all historical cases that have been completed has reached 93%. Because the average length of litigation is between 2.5 and 3 years, the overall internal rate of return (IRR) comes to 27%.

According to Burford Capital's own reports, we know that 75% of all its completed cases have ended in settlement agreements (with ROIC 65%, IRR 23%), 18% in court decisions (ROIC 245%, IRR 49%), and 7% in defeat (ROIC −85%). Burford also publishes ROIC and IRR figures according to individual years in which it has taken on cases for funding. It can be seen from this data that Burford's historical performance is not a matter of one or two lucky periods but that it has been consistently and convincingly excellent over the long term, albeit with relatively large variations from year to year. That is of course understandable in this type of business where the timing and outcome of individual cases cannot be precisely estimated.

How to Value Burford Capital Shares

How should an investor look at Burford and its business? Burford Capital is essentially an investment company, something of a private equity firm, where the individual investments in its portfolio are made up not of equity stakes in companies but of individual court cases numbering in the hundreds. These, when concluded and settled, produce cash flows that Burford reinvests again and again in more and more cases. Let's understand two key points here: how the court cases in the portfolio are valued and what returns can be expected from Burford's investment portfolio and from the company as a whole. When Burford takes on a court case and takes it over from its client, it generally pays the client for the case. Let's say its $20 million. At that point, the case is recorded in the books at acquisition cost, a valuation of $20 million. In the course of litigation, it is common for Burford to accrue costs incrementally and for the valuation of the case to increase by the amounts of those costs. If, say, over the next two years Burford spends a further $3 million on the case, it is valued in the books at $23 million. As the litigation progresses through the various stages, such as preparation, discovery, motions, trial, judgment, appeal, final judgment or agreement, and recovery or settlement, it gradually becomes clearer as to what the court is likely to decide, the probability of the possible outcomes, and when this will happen. Burford may also reflect this into the accounting valuation of the case. At the time the final judgment and its monetary value are known and settled, then the case itself disappears from the books and is replaced by the cash received. In the event of a defeat, only the previous valuation of the case is written off the books and a loss is recorded.

This accounting approach is prescribed by accounting rules and is essentially no different from the accounting of most private equity funds. Private equity funds, like Burford, hold assets in their portfolios that are not publicly traded, have no market prices, and are therefore valued using a particular valuation model. History shows that Burford is very conservative in valuing open litigation cases, and the final judgment in most cases results in an upward revaluation of those cases. When Burford's shares began trading on the New York Stock Exchange in 2020 and the U.S. SEC became its local regulator, the SEC even accused Burford of accounting too conservatively and forced the company to add a time factor into the valuation. In contrast to conventional private equity funds, which have longer life spans and can often value individual investments in a portfolio using a model over a long number of years, the average duration of litigation that Burford has in its portfolio is less than 3 years, and therefore the modeled valuation is replaced very early on by actual cash received. There is then no further uncertainty on the matter of valuation.

As I wrote earlier, the total return on invested capital (ROIC) on all historical closed cases was approximately 93%. This result, by the way, does not include the litigation with Argentina, which is still ongoing. If it ends as I expect (i.e., with a settlement), then the ROIC will probably not be on the order of tens of percent, not even on the order of hundreds of percent, but probably on the order of thousands of percent. Because of its size, it will also significantly affect the overall historical average of concluded cases. Let's not get ahead of ourselves, however, and just assume that an ROIC of 93% is a good indicator of what returns on capital can be expected for Burford in the future. For investors, the ROIC figure is interesting and important, but for valuation of the company itself, it is the IRR that should be used. There is a big difference between an investment that yields an ROIC of 93% in 1 year and one that yields it in 10 years. The time factor and the time value of money are better represented by the IRR. This has historically been 27% for Burford, which corresponds to an average litigation length of just under 3 years. Put simply, Burford Capital can be viewed as an investment portfolio that yields 27% per annum.

The company's equity will not grow at this rate, however. Two additional important elements come into play. The first is the impact of borrowed money, and the second is that of operating costs. Burford is working with long-term debt. The cost of borrowing money is measured in single-digit percentage terms, which is much less than the returns that this capital generates when it is invested into litigation. Financial leverage accelerates the growth of the company's equity capital to rates beyond the IRRs achieved in litigation. In contrast, the growth in equity is reduced by the company's operating expenses, of which personnel costs make up the largest component, and by the dividend that Burford pays to shareholders. You can build a model yourself, playing with the basic variables, which are litigation IRRs, the size of debt, the cost of debt, the size of the dividend, and the company's operating expenses, and then try to estimate how fast the company's equity can grow over the long term. Even with conservative assumptions, you'll probably arrive at a figure of 15–20% per year. This number could be even higher if Burford's management were to take advantage of low stock prices to buy back shares. So far, it has not decided to do so and has always preferred to invest further into new lawsuits, even though it can easily be demonstrated that share buybacks would be a more efficient use of capital. Perhaps the situation in this regard will change for the better once the size and timing of cash flow from the Argentina litigation become clear.

When valuing a financial company, the key metrics for me are most often the amount of equity and its long-term expected growth. The faster the company's equity grows, which means the higher its long-term return on equity (ROE), the higher the multiple of book value that I am willing to assign to it in the valuation. An ROE of 15–20% specifically for Burford means that I would see the intrinsic value of the company somewhere in the range of 1.5–2× book value. I am aware that the wild card in estimating Burford Capital's fundamental value is currently the litigation with Argentina, primarily due to its size. Again, one can model several variants as to how and when this litigation will be settled and see how it translates into the valuation of the company. You might come to the same conclusion that I do, which is that, even if using cautious and conservative expectations regarding the dispute with Argentina, Burford Capital's shares are significantly undervalued. I'm not at all surprised by that undervaluation, because they have every conceivable basis for being so. Passive investors will avoid Burford shares because they are included in almost no major indices. It was only on July 1, 2024, that they were included into the broader Russell 3000 index and into the Russell 2000 index of smaller companies. With a market capitalization of just under $3 billion, Burford is among the smaller companies. It is traded on London's secondary market, AIM, and in the United States only from autumn 2020. These are the sort of classic reasons why passively invested money will almost entirely miss Burford. But there are other hurdles for active investors, too. Burford's type of business is either new or wholly unknown to most investors. Burford is the only major publicly traded litigation finance company. Its analysis requires no small amount of effort and abstract thinking skills. Burford Capital's product is not tangible or visible. Its financial results in each reporting quarter are not, and cannot be, regular. These depend upon, among other things, the cadence with which the results of individual court cases come in, and that cannot be well predicted. It is necessary to reflect on the long term and to have confidence in the ability of management. These are all difficulties that will discourage most investors who might, with a little effort, come to the conclusion that they are looking at a very attractive investment opportunity, one that is almost completely uncorrelated with developments in the economy, and one in which the most important element, the human factor, is involved with almost 100% purity in the creation of value.

Chapter 6

Stellantis

Seeking Treasure in a Company That Everybody Underestimates

The best investments are not in stocks that everyone praises but in stocks that everyone underestimates. That, in one sentence, sums up our investment in Stellantis. This company is itself young, but its individual components have long and interesting histories. I will briefly describe how the company came to be. In 2009, the American carmaker Chrysler went through bankruptcy, and the Italian automaker Fiat became one of the main shareholders, at that time with a 20% stake. Under the leadership of its CEO Sergio Marchionne, Fiat gradually increased its holding until in 2014 it came to own 100% of the shares. The newly formed company, called Fiat Chrysler, began trading on the stock exchange. It was clearly underestimated by the market (including by us) even then, but the stock has done well since – especially when one adds in the performance of Ferrari, which was spun off from Fiat Chrysler in 2016.

Two years later, Marchionne died and John Elkann, the grandson of Gianni Agnelli (Fiat) and CEO of Exor, the main shareholder of Fiat Chrysler, became the prime mover of events. In 2021, Elkann initiated a merger of Fiat Chrysler with the French carmaker Peugeot, thereby creating Stellantis, the fourth-largest car company in the world. Ownership control is held by the Agnelli (via Exor) and Peugeot families. The company's CEO is the highly respected automotive veteran Carlos Tavares.

Déjà Vu?

We think we are once again looking at a situation where the market is underestimating the Stellantis stock. Consider it for yourself: Stellantis is a solid business. It has some of the highest – if not the highest – margins in its industry, and that is before savings from the integration of Peugeot and Fiat Chrysler are fully realized. Return on equity in 2023 was 24.3%, and return on invested capital was 16.5%, double the average for the automotive sector as a whole. This is a decently profitable and financially strong company. We also can find on its balance sheet net cash (cash minus debt) of more than €20 billion. Strong free cash flow allows Stellantis to pay dividends and to repurchase its own shares at a combined rate that exceeds 10% of its market capitalization without reducing its net cash. Asset allocation may be regarded as very good.

The individual Stellantis brands (Alfa Romeo, Chrysler, Citroen, Dodge, Fiat, Jeep, Maserati, Ram, Opel, Lancia, Vauxhall, Peugeot, and others) cover the various market segments, from the low end to luxury, as well as different regions. Peugeot is strong, for example, in France, Germany, and Britain, but also in Argentina. Fiat sells well in Italy, but also in Brazil. We consider the management to be excellent and the controlling shareholders to be very responsible. That all looks good. So, what is the market telling us through the share price? The stock was trading at three times annual earnings in the spring of 2023 when we bought Stellantis shares. If we subtract net cash, which is close to half the market capitalization, we come to 1.5 times annual earnings. That valuation is, in a word, crazy. Add to that a dividend yield of 8.5%, plus share buybacks, and the stock would still be cheap even at twice the price. All in all, after 15 years of watching developments, we had run out of excuses not to buy the stock. We felt like we were experiencing *déjà vu*, something similar to what we had experienced a decade earlier with Fiat Chrysler. It had been a mistake not to buy those shares then, and it could be the same mistake today with the new Stellantis shares. We did not want to underestimate a good company again and ignore the absurdly cheap valuation of its shares.

I use the words *absurdly cheap* because the low price of Stellantis shares defied reason. It was contrary to common sense. If a stock is trading at three times its annual earnings, then the market assumes that those earnings are only temporarily high and that they will soon fall dramatically or that the company is merely surviving, burdened with huge debt, and that it will disappear completely within a few years. This is essentially implicit in the price of a share that trades at three times its annual earnings. If one were to look at the company itself, however, the reality was quite different. Stellantis was not burdened with a lot of debt. On the contrary. It had net cash of more than half its market capitalization. So, its enterprise value (EV), defined as market capitalization + debt − cash, was significantly smaller than its market capitalization alone, and the stock was trading at only 1.5 times EV. Nor did a look at the company's profitability show it to be facing any existential challenges. It was very profitable, and its margins were among the highest in the automotive sector in 2023. Only Ferrari and Porsche, which are automakers in a slightly different product category, had higher margins, and Stellantis scarcely is in competition with those brands.

Imagine yourself owning a company that had a global footprint, was one of the best in the world in terms of size and profitability, was consistently highly profitable, and could make several billion euros more each year on top of its current large amount of cash. Would you be willing to sell it for 3 times the annual profit and even just 1.5 times the EV? I would think certainly not. That price would probably strike you as absurdly low, and a private transaction representing sale of the entire company would not happen at that price. If there were to be a transaction and sale of the entire company, the price would have to be much higher. The public stock markets, therefore, allow to us do something that probably would not be possible at all in a private transaction: to buy a stake in a company at a price that does not even remotely reflect the situation and potential of that enterprise. This is the greatest appeal of stock markets.

The Future of the Automotive Sector

In my opinion, Stellantis' share price signals a big difference between the market's perception of the company and the reality. So, what are the market's perceptions, and what is the reality? Put simply, there is a widespread belief among investors that in the near future all or almost all cars will be electric and if a car company was not already producing electric cars 10 years ago and is therefore one of the so-called "legacy OEMs," who have been making cars for decades and have established operations but face challenges from new entrants and technology car companies, then they have no place in the world, will soon vanish, and deserve neither investors' attention nor their money. You may think I'm exaggerating a bit, but I've heard and read this view mindlessly parroted so many times that there's no need to exaggerate at all. The reality is different from this belief, however, and our thinking about the future of the automotive market needs to be much more sophisticated.

In the past, factors such as global size, brand strength and customer loyalty, product quality, and leadership in the largest markets have determined which car companies will be successful. This always has been a competitive environment, one that has been constantly changing and that has never given anyone a free lunch, as it were. This is still the case today, but new factors are emerging that are disrupting the existing order. I would include among these the pressure to introduce electric cars; changing customer expectations; deglobalization or, if you like, regionalization; and the rise of China.

Perhaps the biggest change, but also the biggest risk, is the pressure for electrification. It is a risk not only for the older car companies that started with electrification later but also for the newer ones that do not even produce cars of other types. The pressure for electrification comes not primarily from customers but from governments that are forcing car manufacturers, often by drastic means, to produce electric cars at the expense of other engine types and that are bribing customers with large subsidies to buy electric cars. Even as this push for electrification is very strong, at the same time it introduces a great deal of risk into the sector. The governments' positions are sometimes strictly dogmatic, but in other circumstances they are pragmatic and open to change according to political developments. Demands for change sometimes accelerate, sometimes slow down, sometimes change direction, and so forth. All this brings a great deal of uncertainty to all car manufacturers at a considerable cost to consumers and to the governments themselves.

Against this backdrop of global pressure for electrification, a strong and competitive automotive sector has sprung up in China. China does not take cautious baby steps. When it ventures into something, big things happen. At a cost of enormous sums of money spent by the Chinese state to support the development of electric car production (even as, ironically, 60–70% of China's electricity comes from burning coal), China has emerged as a strong competitor to global car companies. China is currently enjoying a cost advantage (largely thanks to state subsidies), and it also produces technologically superior products. Its expansion in foreign markets has so far been hampered by poor brand awareness, absence of a distribution and sales network, and weak after-sales support. But these things may soon change. Questions remain as to the extent Chinese exports of electric cars will be hampered by export tariffs in the EU and the United States and how Chinese carmakers will themselves cope with having built up large overcapacity in their home market.

Stellantis is sometimes accused of sleeping through electrification. But this was not a case of oversleeping. It was a conscious decision to stand by and see how things developed before switching to electric cars. This reduced the risk considerably, and from today's perspective, where we are seeing a significant slowing in the adoption of electric cars by customers, thereby forcing individual manufacturers to reassess their original investment plans, it was a good decision. I also appreciate that Stellantis management did not succumb to the oft-seen corporate imperative whereby it could have rushed headlong into something just because others were doing it. Rather, it was able to think independently and was not afraid to take a different approach. Stellantis didn't want to throw billions and billions of euros into making electric cars at a time when that market was tiny, when the manner of pressuring for their manufacture was still being formulated, when it wasn't clear how customers would embrace these vehicles, when electric cars were not price competitive, and when they couldn't compete with internal combustion engine vehicles even on their profit margins. It was only when the market shifted and became a little clearer on all these points that Stellantis went full steam ahead with the development and production of electric cars. The company had one big advantage at the time: it knew what its competitors' products looked like. I regard the whole matter as legitimate and rational positioning. Stellantis certainly didn't oversleep to miss anything. Today, it has more than 45 different battery electric vehicle (BEV) models on the market, and by 2027 that number will exceed 70. In the meantime, Stellantis has been making record profits.

Electrification is far from the only factor affecting the automotive sector. Also important is how customer expectations are changing and, above all, how these expectations differ between the generations, among customers with different incomes or wealth, and in individual parts of the world. We are witnessing a deglobalization of the automotive market together with its increasing fragmentation and customers segmentation. There is no one-size-fits-all solution. Nowadays, it is difficult to predict how the world will evolve. For car companies, this means they need to be flexible if they want to succeed. Stellantis meets this requirement both by having 14 different brands (15 if you include Leapmotor in China) and, above all, by betting on what it terms a "multi-energy platform strategy." This means it can be agnostic in terms of which engine types customers will prefer. Indeed, it can build electric cars, hybrid cars, and internal combustion engine cars on the same production lines. As a global company, it can to a large extent also manufacture them directly where they will be sold.

In such a world, a successful car company must be, in the words of Carlos Tavares, a "local hero" in each of the global market's various bubbles. It must play a leading role in each bubble. For local markets, this means leaning effectively on its global assets, technology, and development. For each bubble it needs to have the right brands, the right products, and the right engine types. (BMW has a similar strategy, which it terms "local for local.") Stellantis has a strong position in two of the three major global markets: North America and Europe. These are followed in importance by a successful and highly profitable market that includes the Middle East and Africa, Latin America, India, and the Pacific part of Asia. Stellantis also has a successful commercial vehicle segment that is perhaps the largest and most profitable in the world. Within Stellantis itself, that segment is above-average profitable and is much less exposed to uncertainty regarding the types of engines that customers want and will want. In this very large and important market segment that is sometimes overlooked by investors, Stellantis is the market leader in Europe, Latin America, and the Middle East. In North America, it is number three in the market.

In China, Stellantis has so far had a minimal position. This might be seen as a negative, but also as a positive. It is positive in the sense that it has enabled Stellantis effectively to enter the Chinese market in 2024 in what can be called an "asset-light" manner. That is to say, with little capital investment. Stellantis bought a one-fifth stake in the Chinese carmaker Leapmotor for just $1 billion. Leapmotor is China's number-three electric car startup. It has products that are competitively priced (currently having about a 30% cost advantage over non-Chinese competitors) and use advanced technology. Stellantis will participate in its further development, sales in China, and exports outside of China. Leapmotor International has been set up for exports and is 51% owned by Stellantis. Some of the Leapmotor cars for export will be manufactured directly in China, and some will be assembled on Stellantis's production lines outside China. This will leverage Stellantis's global manufacturing capabilities to efficiently meet local market demands, as well as to help Stellantis and Leapmotor avoid export restrictions and tariffs on Chinese cars being imposed in Europe and North America.

I think one can see that considerations as to what the automotive market of the future will look like, which car companies will succeed in it, and what they will need to do so are much broader and more complex than how they are often approached. Investors frequently make a mistake here in their thinking, one that is quite common and is repeated time and time again. They underestimate the power of competition. This is an error that applies not only to car companies. It occurs in different sectors and regarding companies of different sizes and developmental stages. It is committed both by companies' management and by investors. All companies face competition. Nothing is free, and nothing is certain. History is replete with examples where even companies in seemingly unshakeable positions have lost their places to competition. Among the most famous examples, I would include companies such as Kodak, Nokia, Xerox, Blockbuster, JC Penney, Blackberry, MySpace, Polaroid, Netscape, and others. On the other hand, there exist a number of cases, too, of companies that looked like they were going to be driven out of the market by competition but that managed to reinvent themselves, adapted to the new environment, and are doing very well today. These include Apple, Netflix, Lego, YouTube, Berkshire Hathaway, LG, American Express, and Corning, to name a few.

Even in the case of car companies, which operate in a competitive environment and in an industry that changes frequently, I would be cautious about condemning some established companies or, conversely, automatically assuming success for other companies. The automotive industry has always been competitive and changing. A lot of formerly existing car companies have either disappeared completely or now exist within larger entities into which they have been merged through gradual consolidation in the industry. The fact that a car company is today success-ful, large, profitable, and among the sector's leaders is no guarantee of future success. This does mean, on the other hand, that such a firm has been able to establish itself successfully through the decades in a very tough environment. Their success heretofore also is not to be ignored and may be a certain signal for the future. If, for example, companies such as Toyota or BMW have been able to demonstrate longtime leadership in the automotive sector, whether that be in terms of technology, quality, management systems, or profit margins, they are best positioned to remain leaders. Conversely, many new automotive startups whose emergence is accompanied by investor optimism have not yet proven that they are capable to weather a competitive and rapidly changing environment.

Coming back to Stellantis, its relatively short history suggests that this is a well-run company with management aware of what it should be doing, having a clear strategy that it can execute, and with a visible track record of doing just that. A brief review of the past 15 years will provide sufficient evidence: The takeover of Chrysler after bankruptcy and its merger with Fiat. The spin-off of Ferrari into a separate company. The merger with Peugeot and creation of what is now Stellantis. Transition to a single manufacturing platform for all engine types. The ability to invent and apply a proprietary and industry-unique method of introducing electric car production. Entry into the Chinese market in a manner that has relatively low capital requirements. These are major steps changing the face of the company and at the same time moving it significantly forward. For each of these, management has had to face skepticism from investors. The result, however, has always been better than expected. It is fair to say that Stellantis has been repeatedly, and perhaps unfairly, undervalued over the past 15 years. This is reflected in its share price, which often is attractively low.

From an investment point of view, it is interesting to look for cases of companies regarding which investors' perceptions diverge markedly from reality. This is a relatively common phenomenon, and it is to be expected that, in an environment where markets are dominated by passive forms of investment, there will be no shortage of such situations. Of course, mismatch between investors' subjective perceptions and objectively existing reality can go either way. Perceptions can be both much worse than reality and much better than reality. Undervaluation of companies then leads to cheap share prices, while overvaluation leads to overpriced shares. Cheap and expensive are meant here relative to the intrinsic values of specific companies. As investors, we are more interested in situations where stocks are underappreciated. These may be considered as candidates for addition to a portfolio. It is also a good thing, however, to be able to recognize when stocks are significantly overvalued and to steer well clear of them.

Cash Is King

When we finally got around to buying Stellantis shares in the spring of 2023 (yes, we actually ran out of excuses not to buy the stock), they were very cheap. The entire company had a market capitalization of around €45 billion and held net cash of near €26 billion, equal to almost 60% of its market capitalization. There was no doubt that the shares were extremely cheap relative to the profits the company was currently making. A P/E of around 3×, a P/EV of around 1.5×, and free cash flow yield (FCFY) of almost 20% spoke volumes. One rarely sees similar values for fundamental valuation metrics. Nonetheless, that would not necessarily mean that something is an attractive investment. Indeed, the value of any investment is the sum of all future cash flows (discounted back to the present), and the past has no role to play. One would therefore have to ask whether Stellantis's future will be better than the share price suggests. We could have asked that question, but we asked a different question, inspired by Charlie Munger, Warren Buffett's longtime partner at Berkshire Hathaway. Munger was still alive and mentally quite spry at an incredible 99 years of age when we bought Stellantis stock. He was renowned for his wisdom and left behind many great *bon mots* and ideas.

Probably the most celebrated of Munger's sayings goes like this: "All I want to know is where I'm going to die so I'll never go there." This, of course, was meant in jest and is not a wish that could be fulfilled. Nevertheless, it is a statement inspired by the same great Prussian mathematician, Jacobi, who advised "Invert, always invert!" as a tool for solving difficult problems. It was precisely the advice "Invert, always invert!" that at one time made the greatest impression upon me. I no longer remember the first time I heard it. Perhaps it was 20 or 30 years ago, but I would say it still holds the top position among Mungerisms. Maybe it reminds me a little nostalgically of my secondary school years when we covered proof by contradiction in my beloved math class, but the "Invert, always invert!" approach can be applied generally to problem-solving in almost any field of thought. It seeks to strive for good judgment mainly by collecting instances of bad judgment and then contemplating ways to avoid such outcomes. In the case of Stellantis, and in the spirit of Munger's quote, we asked ourselves how much and how quickly Stellantis would have to begin to collapse completely as a business in order to justify the existing extreme cheapness of its stock. Did there exist any realistic scenario with significant probabilities wherein Stellantis could expect such a dramatically negative development? We have assumed that there is not.

When we put together the current state of Stellantis, its high margins, high profitability, strong balance sheet, model lineup spanning almost the entire price spectrum, use of diverse motor types, and coverage of varied customer needs, and then took into account the medium-term plans that management had presented in its Dare Forward 2030 program, we made our own calculations as to possible future profitability and also took into account the consensus among analysts who follow Stellantis. Our resulting picture was different from the apparent market view. Realistically, by the end of this decade (i.e., 2030), Stellantis can be expected to produce free cash flow that may exceed its market capitalization. This certainly will not be a smooth and uneventful ride, however. We expect both worse times and better times, which is pretty typical for this sector. The year 2024, for example, will turn out much worse than expected for Stellantis, as well as for other automakers. Free cash flow is the cash that the company has left over not only after paying for the costs of conducting its business but also after investing into its development, after investing into its research, after making investments needed for the transition to new motor types, after building new production lines and constructing battery gigafactories, after costs related to the development of new models, and after costs related to the development and investment into new and additional services (concerning the circular economy, data, mobility, financial services, the used car market, autonomous driving), and so on. After all these expenses, Stellantis's free cash flow could by the end of 2030 still reach tens of billions of euros cumulatively. Paradoxically, how management handles this huge sum will have greater impact on shareholder value than whether the actual amount of free cash flow is a few billion higher or lower. Efficient capital allocation is perhaps even more important here than is the business itself.

If Stellantis will squander this amount on overpriced acquisitions or for other nonsensical purposes, that will have a very negative impact on its stock value. But if it uses this money in ways that increase shareholder value for existing shareholders, then Stellantis will make its stock even more attractive. With a view to the management itself, we believe Stellantis is in excellent hands. We consider its CEO, Carlos Tavares, to be one of the best managers in the auto industry, if not the best ever. Tavares's career of 40+ years in the automotive sector has seen him build a sterling track record in restructuring Peugeot, Citroen, DS, and the European arm of Opel (following its acquisition from GM), as well as the creation of Stellantis through the merger of Fiat Chrysler and Peugeot. These are all some of the most notable performances within the automotive sector in the past 20 years. (Note: Tavares's contract as CEO at Stellantis expires in 2026, and we expect a new CEO to come in. John Elkann should have the final word on that person's selection.)

For the most fundamental and most important capital allocation decisions in relation to shareholder value, however, we need to look a level higher in the company's hierarchy, namely, to its shareholder structure. The largest shareholder is the company Exor, with approximately 15% of the equity and an even slightly larger voting interest. Exor is a holding company controlled by the Italian Agnelli family through the private company Giovanni Agnelli BV. Exor is headed by John Elkann, a grandson of Giovanni Agnelli. John Elkann is a well-known name among value stock investors. The way in which he has been running Exor since 2011 shows unambiguously that his first concern is the creation of shareholder value. The transactions he concludes and the results they produce make Exor shareholders happy. Stellantis is Exor's largest and most important investment, and it is very fitting that the person who has and will have a major say in the asset allocation at Stellantis is John Elkann. As Stellantis shareholders, the Tavares–Elkann combination strikes us as ideal for value creation, and this played a key role in our decision to buy. So far, we are pleased with the asset allocation at Stellantis. Since the spring of 2023, when Stellantis substantially raised its annual dividend, as it did again in spring 2024, we've recovered about 20% of our original purchase price in dividends alone. In addition, the company has since repurchased more than 9% of its own shares at prices corresponding to P/Es between 3× and 5×. At these share prices, repurchases have a significantly positive impact on value creation, and we cannot help but wish that the share price stays this low for as long as possible. Stellantis has no intention of letting up in returning excess cash to shareholders.

Of all the stocks discussed in this book, Stellantis is the one most likely to prove our reasoning to be incorrect. We are aware of this, and the size of this position in the portfolio corresponds to that understanding. The year 2024 was the first since Carlos Tavares took over at PSA (before Stellantis was formed) that he had to significantly reduce his own initial profitability projections during the year. Ours is a contrarian investment, and we well know that we are in a minority with this view. That, however, doesn't bother us, and we have no reason up to now to reassess our investment. Time will tell whether Stellantis is a hidden investment treasure and a good investment at a share price of €12.

Chapter 7

Jungfraubahn

Seeking Treasure Among Tourism Monopolies

Every year I have a yearbook sent to me from Switzerland. Its subtitle translates to "The Indispensable Working Tool for Every Investor." It lists all titles traded on the Zurich Stock Exchange. Each company is given an entire page, and basic information is presented in a clear manner. I like to browse such publications because I can get a fairly quick overview of a given market and might occasionally even come across an interesting investment opportunity. We rarely see this in Switzerland, because the Swiss equities market, together with the Danish market, has long been one of the most expensive in the world. Still, it's worth watching, and not long ago this even paid off for us. In 2021, while flipping through the yearbook, I came across a company called Jungfraubahn, which led somewhat later to our next investment.

At 4,158 meters above sea level, Jungfrau is the tallest peak of the mountain massif of the same name in the Bernese Alps region. Together with the Eiger and Mönch peaks, they form a magnificent triad, and the view of them is one of the most beautiful in the Alps. When I was just a kid climbing rocks, I devoured books about conquering the north face of the Eiger. It is 1,800 meters high, and, because of its length, steepness, and dangerous combination of ice and rock, it long resisted attempts by those who would climb it. It was only in 1938 that a group of four Austrian and German climbers finally succeeded. One member of this group was Heinrich Harrer. A few years before the adventures chronicled in his *Seven Years in Tibet*, Harrer wrote a great book about the conquest of the Eiger, *The White Spider*. Sometime in the mid-1990s, when I was on holiday in Switzerland with my wife and our first daughter, we rode together a cog railway, its route leading through a tunnel in the Eiger massif to the Jungfraujoch saddle at 3,454 meters above sea level. Suddenly, you find yourself in another world. Icy air smacks your face, the snow crunches underfoot, and the panorama almost takes your breath away: on one side a view of the Swiss plateau all the way to France, on the other the Aletsch Glacier contained within the valleys below 4,000-meter peaks. It was a wonderful experience that remains etched in our minds.

So, when I came across the name of the company Jungfraubahn, it was immediately clear to me what this was all about. Jungfraubahn Holding AG owns and operates the railway that we once took to the Jungfraujoch. Moreover, a graph of the company's stock price caught my eye. In 2020, Jungfraubahn's stock price recorded the biggest drop in its history, and we wondered if this created a good investment opportunity. We decided to dive into Jungfraubahn in detail.

Tourism's Diversity

The tourism industry is quite large and includes a wide range of companies. Some of them are built directly on tourism and travel; others are indirectly affected by it. In many cases, these are companies well known to the public, and they may present a number of both obvious as well as altogether inconspicuous investment opportunities for investors. Companies that have built their businesses directly on travel include, for example, hotel chains (Marriott International, Hilton Worldwide

Holdings), travel agencies (TUI AG), booking and accommodation services companies (Booking Holdings, Expedia Group, Airbnb), cruise lines (Royal Caribbean Cruises, Carnival Corporation, Norwegian Cruise Line Holdings), and so on. For many other companies, travel and tourism is not the only source of revenue, but it is nevertheless a substantial one. Here I would name, for example, airlines, various types of land and sea transport, car rental companies, companies providing catering services, reservation services, and tourist attractions. This is a diverse sector that on the whole has been growing significantly over the long term. Its various subsectors have different economic characteristics, and the companies apply diverse business models. There are companies whose business models place relatively low demands on capital (Hilton Worldwide Holdings) and companies whose demands are very high (cruise lines). There are narrowly defined business models (Booking Holdings) and more complex models (The Walt Disney Company). We find companies where it is easier to build upon brand strength (Airbnb) and companies where it is difficult to create a sustainable competitive advantage (airlines). There exist companies that are solely in the domestic travel business, as well as companies that are in the inbound tourism business and others that handle outbound travel. I could go on and on with this division and categorization, but we will be interested in the category known as tourist attractions.

Tourist attractions are a magnet for tourists, one of the main motivations for getting off the couch and going somewhere. From a business point of view, they provide an opportunity to build a source of income around them. I would divide them into several groups. The first consists of attractions built by people. Most of them were not built originally for tourists but originated as a by-product of historical development. Some of the most visited in the world are the Forbidden City in Beijing, St Peter's Basilica at the Vatican, the castle at Versailles, and the Acropolis in Athens. A second group consists of natural attractions created by nature itself. Among the most visited in the world are the Grand Canyon in Arizona, Table Mountain in Cape Town, Moraine Lake in Canada, Ha Long Bay in Vietnam, or Switzerland's Zermatt and the Matterhorn. Millions of people a year visit each of these, thereby becoming clients of tourism companies in virtually all subcategories. A third group then consists of attractions that are built by people and are directly intended to be destinations for entertainment tourism. The best examples of this group are the Disneyland resorts, of which there are several around the world (Florida, Paris, Shanghai, Tokyo, etc.).

When I think of the Jungfraubahn as a business based on combining travel with a very attractive tourist destination, a comparison that always comes to mind is the Eiffel Tower in Paris. With 7 million visitors a year, it is one of the world's top 10 human-made attractions. The Eiffel Tower ticks all the boxes. It lies in a city that is itself a magnet for tourists and is the most frequently displayed symbol of Paris. It lies in the very center of the city, it provides a spectacular view of Paris, and going to its top can be associated for many people with the feeling that they have done something extraordinary. From a business perspective, the Eiffel Tower is a local monopoly, and, while there are competing sites that can attract tourist attention (the Louvre, Versailles, the Champs Élysées), Paris has no other comparable attraction and probably will not have one any time soon. Built in 1889, the Eiffel Tower is now owned by the city and operated by the *Société d'Exploitation de la Tour Eiffel*, which is also 99% owned by the city. In 2022, the company's revenues totaled €113 million, and royalties paid to the City of Paris came to around €16 million. It's a nice little business that is de facto guaranteed an annual influx of customers. There is little to threaten its exceptional position, but, on the other hand, it is limited in terms of further development.

Local Monopoly

The Jungfraubahn has the same advantages as the Eiffel Tower, but at the same time it has room for further growth and development. In 1893, the Swiss industrialist Adolf Guyer-Zeller requested permission to build a cog railway from Wengernalp station (1,874 m a.s.l.) through Kleine Scheidegg to the summit of the Jungfrau (3,454 m a.s.l.). The route was to run through a tunnel inside the Eiger and Mönch mountains. Construction began in 1896 and was completed in 1912. This was the origin of the Jungfraubahn company. This railway line is still in use today and is the core of the business, and that business has been gradually expanded to include other products and services. What induced Adolf Guyer-Zeller to build a railway through the middle of a mountain and a railway station at a height that has not been surpassed in Europe since? It must have been the natural beauty of the location. Just as the city of Paris provided the ideal space for constructing the Eiffel Tower and its subsequent commercial exploitation, the Eiger, Mönch, and Jungfrau massifs are ideal for hiking. It is one of the most beautiful places in the Alps and easily accessible. It is sometimes said that in real estate the three most important factors are "location, location, and location." If the Eiffel Tower stood not in the center of Paris, but perhaps in the Massif Central, it would have only a fraction of the visitors that it does.

Like the Eiffel Tower, the Jungfraubahn benefits from a local monopoly. There are innumerable tourist attractions in the Alps, all of which are in their own way substitutes and competitors, but it is difficult to find a combination that could surpass the Jungfraubahn as regards the appeal of the place itself, its beauty, its accessibility, the ease with which one can reach the heights, its technical attractions, and the developed tourist infrastructure. The company makes good use of all this. From the original cog railway built more than a century ago, a whole tourist complex has sprung up in the area. It is owned and operated by the Jungfraubahn. This is one of the leading tourist-oriented companies in Switzerland and also the largest mountain railway company. In addition to the original railway on the Jungfrau, the company operates and owns other railways and cable cars around Grindelwald and Wengen, ski slopes, lifts and winter sports facilities, a hydroelectric power station, restaurants, shops, and car parks. Putting it all together, and especially because of the cog railway on the Jungfrau, this is perhaps the biggest tourist attraction in the Alps.

I have been visiting the Alps regularly for more than 30 years, several times every winter and also in the summer. In that time, I have noticed three things. First, every year you can see that the tourist resorts are evolving and improving. Each year brings a new lift, a new slope, new snowmaking, new lighting for night skiing, more cross-country ski trails, new accommodations, parking lots, pools, and so on. A second thing that cannot go unnoticed is that everything gets more expensive every year. The most sought-after tourist centers have a great ability to pass on by way of their prices their rising operating costs, higher capital requirements, and notions of acceptable margins. They have great pricing power. The third observation that, again, cannot be overlooked is that it's always crowded. We can expect that not much will change in the future. Tourism will continue to account for a large and, as wealth grows, perhaps an increasingly large, share of families' spending. Tourist centers will continue to accommodate this with their own development, and the last thing I'd worry about is whether prices will rise. Something interesting emerged from a discussion at an investment conference with some investor friends from the United States when I presented our investment into the Jungfraubahn: in a price comparison, it worked out that a day's downhill skiing in the Alps is much cheaper than is a day's skiing at a comparably equipped resort in the United States.

All these things were going through my mind when I came across Jungfraubahn Holding AG while flipping through the yearbook of Swiss stocks and I was wondering why the stock's price had fallen so much and whether it might be a good investment opportunity. The reason for the price decline was obvious. This was in 2021, the second year that COVID was raging in Europe and lockdowns were disrupting economies. The Jungfraubahn's business, too, was paralyzed at that time. The Jungfraubahn is essentially a year-round business, but it has two logical seasonal peaks: the ski season in winter and the main tourist season in summer. During the lockdown, tourism was limited, even impossible in some places, and the Jungfraubahn's income was hit hard.

The winter and summer seasons differ for the Jungfraubahn, not least because winter sports are the main activities in winter and summer is more about regular tourism. It also differs in that winter visitors come in large numbers individually. Most of them come from Switzerland and other European countries. Summer visitors, on the other hand, come largely through organized group tours, and Asian tourists play an important role. In 2019, the last normal year for tourism before the pandemic, more than 1 million tourists traveled to the Jungfraujoch during the summer season, and the number of visitors to the Jungfraubahn complex during the winter season also exceeded 1 million. A year later, everything was different. On March 14, 2020, the resorts were closed, winter tourists disappeared from the region almost overnight, and summer tourists did not come. It was to be expected that this would have a negative impact on the Jungfraubahn's sales and profits. Revenues dropped from CHF 223 million in 2019 to CHF 125 million in 2020; from a profit of CHF 53 million, the company fell into a loss of CHF 9 million. Moreover, at that time, no one knew what would happen next. Switzerland had one of the loosest movement regimes during the pandemic, so at least a limited number of domestic tourists were on the slopes around the Eiger during summer and winter. International tourism stopped almost completely, however, and Jungfraubahn reports that organized tours for tourists from Asia ceased altogether.

Tourism remained in a deep slump during 2021. The number of winter visitors was even lower than the year before, and the number of summer visitors remained just as bad as in 2020. The company adapted somewhat to the continuing depression and, with revenues of CHF 130 million, ended with a profit of zero and a much-improved, albeit still negative, cash flow. The share price, which had plunged to CHF 100 in the darkest times in October 2020 from about CHF 165 just before the pandemic broke, remained relatively low despite a slight recovery and even gradually fell again during 2022 after publication of the 2021 results. In terms of the pandemic, however, 2022 was no longer so depressing as had been 2021 or even 2020. It was increasingly clear that the pandemic's end was near and that life would gradually return to normal in all its forms. In the first half of March 2023, I was at the cross-country ski races in St. Moritz and could see with my own eyes that tourism was once again in full swing and approaching the pre-2020 figures. The Jungfraubahn's still-low share price was thus a step behind the world's developments. When we bought the shares in the second half of March 2023 at 130 francs, the price was lower than it had been for most of 2021, which didn't make much sense. In the end, it also turned out that 2023 really did bring a return to normal and that the number of visitors to the Jungfraujoch in summer and the number of visitors to the region in winter both exceeded 1 million. Revenues in that year reached CHF 278 million and profits CHF 79 million. While this is much improved, it still doesn't mean that the company is maximizing its potential. In the coming years, we expect Jungfraubahn to continue on its original path of growth, development, and improvement of its services, thus benefiting from its rather unique position in the tourism sector.

Jungfraubahn is a small company (at the time of our purchase it had a market capitalization of only CHF 750 million), and, as such, its shares make up one of the smallest positions in Vltava Fund's portfolio. It is likely to remain so. Nonetheless, it is a nice asset, and we are pleased with its performance so far. It is a classic example of a company that has been ignored by the market for longer than it deserved, and one where this situation created opportunity to make a good yet low-risk investment. Among companies with small market capitalizations, so-called *small caps*, one can sometimes find interesting hidden investment treasures. Jungfraubahn is a typical small cap. Passive investors will not even care to invest their money into it, because the company is not represented in any major indices. Few active investors seem to know about it, despite that the company's name is readily visible. Interestingly, before and during our buying, the share price was stagnant at CHF 130 francs for quite some time. As soon as we disclosed in a letter to shareholders published on April 4, 2023, that we had purchased Jungfraubahn shares, however, the price immediately began to rise. Where there is low liquidity and a small market capitalization, sometimes it takes little impetus for a share price to begin better to reflect the value of a company. Our letter to shareholders may have contributed to this.

Chapter 8

NVR

Seeking Treasure Among Companies with Low Capital Requirements

The best businesses are those that generate high returns on capital and are able to reinvest the capital earned over the long term with similarly high returns. In these cases, there is rapid capital accumulation due to what is essentially a high compounded rate interest. If an investor manages to discover such a company, it can be profitable to hold onto its shares for the long term. There are few companies of this type, however, mainly because opportunities for long-term reinvestment of capital at high rates of return are rare. A second-best case might be such businesses that generate high returns on capital; can reinvest only relatively small portions of the capital earned at high rates of return, which is what they do; and then return the excess capital to shareholders over the long term in the form of share buybacks. One company that meets those criteria is NVR.

NVR's business is in an industry where we might not expect to find an example of a company achieving high returns on capital over the long term. That industry is homebuilding. Companies in this sector are often disparaged because theirs is a cyclical industry, sensitive to the business cycle and to the level of interest rates. Occasional and more or less inevitable recessions in homebuilding lead to deep slumps in sales, and homebuilders can find themselves in situations where they have large inventories of unsold homes, a lot of capital invested in land that currently seems expensive and unmarketable, and, if they also are saddled with a lot of debt, in a state of hardship imperiling their existence. NVR could tell about this, because it historically has had its own negative but at the same time valuable experience with such difficulties.

New Beginnings and Transformation

In the 1980s, NVR was the quintessential homebuilder and full-fledged land developer. That is to say, on its own account it bought land in a condition not yet ready for house building. These land parcels, then, gradually went through the phases of zone permitting, planning, utilities and infrastructure engineering, and construction. Only after all this could houses be built on them. This process takes several years, ties up a lot of capital, and carries the risk of failing to earn sufficient returns, either in terms of absolute amounts or in relation to the speed at which those returns can be realized. NVR also produced building materials, had its own unit that provided construction financing, and was spread out across too much of the United States in its business. During the economic and construction recession of the early 1990s, NVR had to declare bankruptcy. When it emerged from bankruptcy in 1992, however, it had a business model completely different from its previous one. That model is still in place today and uniquely positions NVR among its competitors. This is the main source of its almost miraculous growth in value per share. Over the past 30 years, NVR's stock has been one of the best-performing U.S. stocks ever.

So, what does NVR's current business model look like? It is based on three fundamental pillars. The first pillar is low capital requirements, the second is an efficient homebuilding process, and the third is highly efficient allocation of capital. We will now discuss all three.

Any company that builds houses needs to have an inventory of land upon which to build in the future. That land bank should be equivalent to several years of the company's normal annual construction development so that it never finds itself facing demand from customers for new houses but no place to build them. This would cause unnecessary loss of turnover and profit for the company. That's why every development company must plan for years ahead, find the necessary land, and acquire it into its ownership. Holding land for several years, though, means that the typical homebuilder will tie up a large amount of capital doing so. This is expensive. The capital is practically frozen for some period of time, often is financed with debt, and is at risk should the value of the land drop. To avoid these risks, NVR almost completely avoids buying land that is not ready for development. Therefore, it need not embark on time- and capital-intensive development itself. Instead, it focuses on buying ready land, and not with cash but through purchase options. The option premium can typically be as high as 10% of the land price, and this alone comprises the capital and risk involved for NVR. Should NVR decide to withdraw from the intended purchase of the land, in the worst case it will lose only the option premium. Not only is this approach less risky and less capital intensive, it also allows NVR to control much more land through options than would be possible in the case of full purchase. For the record, NVR built just more than 20,000 homes in 2023. At the end of 2023, it controlled 141,500 lots, which would be enough for seven years of construction. It spent $584 million on them, which is only about $4,000 per lot on average. It's really a low-cost and efficient way of acquiring land inventory.

The second pillar is the high efficiency of NVR's development process. First, NVR is focused on a few key markets and on building market leadership in those markets. Geographically, it has four major segments: Mid Atlantic (Maryland, Virginia, West Virginia, Delaware, and Washington, D.C.), North East (New Jersey, Eastern Pennsylvania), Mid East (New York, Ohio, Western Pennsylvania, Indiana, and Illinois), and South East (North Carolina, South Carolina, Tennessee, Florida, and Georgia). This is a fairly consolidated market block. In some of these markets, NVR has market share in excess of 20% and can thus benefit from economies of scale. Second, NVR operates factories close to its main markets where it produces prefabricated building components, and this significantly reduces costs. Third, NVR uses independent subcontractors to build its houses, working on fixed-price contracts. This makes NVR's margins more stable. When the construction industry was in crisis in the United States between 2006 and 2011 and the number of new homes built dropped significantly, NVR was the only publicly traded homebuilder that remained profitable and even performed well. Fourth, NVR overwhelmingly builds homes only when they are presold and when the down payment has been made. It does not engage in speculative construction. The risk of NVR being left with a stock of unsold houses in the event of a recession is low. Fifth, NVR offers mortgage financing to its home buyers. The mortgages are not held by NVR after closing, however, but are sold to banks. In this case, NVR's revenue is the closing fee or the profit on the mortgage. This is a smaller segment within NVR, but one with high margins and again with low capital requirements.

The third pillar of NVR's success is highly efficient capital allocation. NVR's established and unique business model is not capital intensive. Holding a land inventory using options requires relatively little capital. The construction method itself, whereby NVR considers itself more of an assembler putting the house together than a builder, also does not require much capital for machinery and equipment. To grow itself, NVR does not pursue acquisitions but rather seeks to grow organically and gradually strengthen its position in existing markets. From there, it then expands progressively into surrounding markets. This, then, is more about logistical and organizational matters than about large capital outlays. The combination of low invested capital needs and high margins relative to its industry results in high returns on invested capital and high returns on incremental invested capital. NVR produces far more capital than it can effectively reinvest back into the existing business and into further growth. Logically, therefore, it does not use much debt financing, and typically we find net cash on the balance sheet. NVR returns surplus capital to shareholders on an ongoing basis in the form of share buybacks. It avoids paying dividends as a taxable and less-efficient form of returning capital and focuses entirely on share buybacks. Remarkably, it has applied this approach since the beginning of its transition to the current business model after emerging from bankruptcy. As a result, the number of NVR shares outstanding has plummeted and continues to fall. At the end of 1995, NVR had 15.2 million shares in circulation. By the end of 2000, this number was down to 8.9 million. At the end of 2010, it was 5.6 million, and today the number is closing in on the 3 million mark. This means that the number of NVR shares has fallen by more than 80% since 1995. We added NVR shares to Vltava Fund's portfolio just before Christmas 2020, and since that time alone the number of NVR shares has fallen by one-fifth. It is important to reiterate that share buybacks are not coming at the cost of greater debt. NVR has more cash than debt, and I don't expect anything to change about this going forward.

To get a sense of just how high NVR's returns on capital are, how low the capital requirements of its business model are, and how much cash it is able to return to shareholders on an ongoing basis, one needs only to look at its 2023 financial statements. From an industry-wide perspective, 2023 was a pretty average year. The total number of homes completed in the United States was 1.4 million. What return on invested capital (ROIC) did NVR achieve? Let's use the formula from Chapter 4 on Alimentation Couche-Tard:

$$ROIC = \frac{Net\ profit}{Invested\ capital}$$

NVR's net profit was \$1.59 billion. The average invested capital during the year (equity + debt − cash) was approximately \$2 billion. The ROIC is therefore almost 80%. Cash flow from operating activities was \$1.5 billion. If we subtract \$99 million that was attributable to stock-based compensation, which should logically fall under the category of cash flow from financing activities, we get \$1.4 billion representing net cash flow from operating activities. Furthermore, the cash flow statement's section on investing activities shows that NVR spent only \$25 million on the purchase of tangible fixed assets, mainly machinery, and equipment. That shows just how low NVR's capital expenditures are. The net free cash flow is therefore scarcely different from the \$1.4 billion achieved through operating activities. This allowed NVR to spend nearly \$1.1 billion on buying back its own shares during 2023 while still ending the year with more cash on hand than it had at the start of the year. It's a great business that has operated this way for more than 30 years and may work the same way for the next 30 years.

The long-term decline in the number of shares outstanding at such a tempo as occurring at NVR is an incredible means of growing a company's value per share. Here are some historical numbers to illustrate this:

In the 15 years from the end of 2008 to the end of 2023, NVR's revenue increased by 1.6 times and its net income by 14.7 times. Revenue per share, however, has risen by 3.5 times and earnings per share by 23.7 times.

NVR is a company with a narrowly focused business and therefore has been strongly influenced by developments in the industry within which it operates. Homebuilding is an industry that is cyclical. See Figure 8.1.

Demand for new home construction is influenced by a number of factors in the short and medium terms. These include mainly employment, real incomes of residents, availability and cost of financing, and house prices. In the long term, population growth, the rate of family formation, and changes in lifestyles are crucial. NVR cannot avoid short-term cyclical influences. That is in fact impossible. Nonetheless, NVR is much more resilient in relation to these impacts than are most of its competitors. This is precisely because of its business model that ensures small land inventories, net cash on its balance sheet, production efficiencies, higher margins, and a strong position in the markets within which NVR operates. As investors in Vltava Fund, we do not avoid cyclical sectors *a priori* if we see a long-term positive trend in the sector and if we find a company having a sustainable competitive advantage within the sector. In our opinion, NVR exactly fits this description.

The secular trend in the homebuilding industry should continue to put wind in NVR's sails. The U.S. population has been growing at a rate of just over 1 million people per year in recent years. (When accounting for illegal migration, this number would have to be much higher.) The Joint Center for Housing Studies at Harvard University estimates that the rate

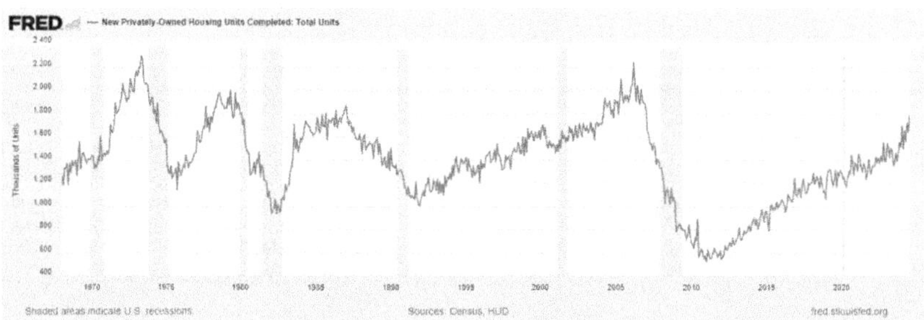

Figure 8.1   New privately owned housing units completed (total units). *Sources:* United States Census Bureau; United States Department of Housing; Urban Development.

of family formation in the United States is currently 1.2 million per year. The Joint Center's studies also estimate that about 1.5 million new homes would need to be built annually to meet demand, which is more than has been built in recent years. (Incidentally, it is estimated that per year about 1% of existing housing units are lost, abandoned, or demolished. In the United States, housing units currently number about 144 million.) Various limitations in planning and permitting are most often cited as the main reasons for supply lagging demand, and the United States is no exception in that regard. We see the same situation in the United Kingdom, for example. We have been following the residential construction market there for more than 20 years, and it also suffers from a chronic shortage of new homes being built compared to what the country's demographics would require. The Czech Republic is in a similar position.

Sources of Competitive Advantage

That NVR's business model has been successful can be seen clearly in its historical results, and its past stock returns are literally phenomenal. At this point, then, a few basic questions naturally arise. First, why isn't NVR's business model followed by more companies in the industry? Second, why are NVR's stock returns consistently so good when its price should theoretically (in the sense of academic investment theory) always reflect its current intrinsic value? Third, what does the future look like?

It is impossible to find definitive and objectively correct answers to these questions, but that doesn't prevent us from speculating about their possible answers. First, why aren't more homebuilders doing this? If there exist companies applying less conventional business models that have performed highly above average or sometimes even been exceptionally successful in their industries over the long term and if their business models are there in front of everyone's eyes and easy to understand, then one would expect them to have many imitators. That would especially be true in cases where the excellence of these companies is not based on some unique product or technological edge. Nevertheless, NVR has no successful imitators among its competitors. While it is true that some competing companies are trying to adopt some individual features from NVR into their own businesses, these are rather incremental attempts. The British company Vistry set out on a course last year that is in some ways similar to the path that NVR is taking, but it hasn't yet gone far down that route, and it's too early to make any judgments. I think the most likely reason why there aren't more NVRs on the market is not that the managements of competing companies don't know the NVR business model, don't recognize it, or arrogantly ignore it. The reason is probably that it is not easy to apply this model. It may not be so straightforward in practice as appears on its surface. I have come to similar conclusions regarding some other longtime extremely successful companies in other industries. We've talked about Berkshire Hathaway, and another example that comes to mind is the Canadian company Constellation Software. Each has a unique business model based on organization, logistics, and philosophy and almost no imitators. If my conjecture as to why these companies have few imitators is correct, then their business models can be seen as sustainable competitive advantages that are likely to be sustained over the long term.

Why are NVR's stock returns consistently so good when, in theory, its price should always reflect its current intrinsic value? Well, first of all, I should reiterate that I don't believe in efficient markets theory. I even would say that we are moving further and further away from the efficient market ideal due to the overwhelming prevalence of passive investing. Still, in the specific case of NVR, there are several possible explanations why the market pays the company less attention than it deserves and why its stock is undervalued most of the time, even though this is one of the best-performing stocks ever over the long term and should therefore be under the scrutiny of investors. NVR is one of the easiest companies to understand, yet its business model remains largely underappreciated by investors. Instead, NVR is seen as just another one of the homebuilders, as a highly cyclical company in an industry where shares typically trade at low earnings multiples and even lower multiples of book value. At first glance, NVR stock may look expensive by this comparison. NVR's average P/E over the past 10 years has been around 15×, according to Value Line, and the current P/BV stands at about /×. Both values are high for the sector. Moreover, NVR does not now and has not ever paid a dividend. That's a minus in some investors' eyes, but it is a good decision and part of an efficient long-term capital allocation. In my eyes, the P/E at 15× is not a hurdle for NVR. In fact, this needs to be seen in the context of high returns on capital and much less cyclicality than for most of its competitors. The earnings multiples at which NVR trades are much lower than are the earnings multiples for the overall market, and yet NVR has an incomparably better set of parameters, such as free cash flow and earnings per share growth in addition to high returns on capital. The P/BV in NVR's case does not indicate expensiveness but rather reflects low capital requirements, which is a valuable attribute and something that we actually want to see in a good company.

Only eight stock analysts cover the company, according to NVR's own information, and just three of those eight firms can be deemed really significant. Moreover, management makes no effort to promote its own shares. It doesn't hold quarterly conference calls, and its quarterly reports are brief. I don't recall NVR ever holding an investor day for investors and analysts, nor does it produce any presentations about itself. Instead, the focus is on the business alone, and even management compensation is geared in that same direction. These may be some of the reasons why the stock of a company like NVR trades at significantly lower earnings multiples than does the U.S. market as a whole, even though it is a substantially above-average company in all major respects.

What can we expect going forward? I think this will be more or less a continuation of past trends. NVR's industry will continue to be highly cyclical, but that should not be a constraint. NVR also weathered a huge drop in residential construction volumes during the 2006–2011 crisis, as we say in Czech, "without losing a flower." It is difficult to imagine a more challenging stress test. In the long run, the deficit between the quantity of houses being built and the quantity demanded by people will likely continue to prevail. Investing is not primarily about finding industries or sectors that are poised to boom, however, but about finding companies that have sustainable competitive advantage. That is exactly the kind of company that NVR is and what I expect it to remain. A hidden investment treasure grounded in a unique business model and complemented by exemplary capital allocation, it should continue to bring shareholders joy and good returns.

Chapter 9

Japan

Seeking Treasure in a Country Most Investors Ignore

We will step away from the search for value in specific companies in this chapter and the next one to describe two examples of the search for value from a macro perspective. In this way, too, we can find differences between ideas and assumptions that the market implicitly displays in share prices and the underlying reality. The first example will be Japan. I will strive to explain why we believed some time ago that Japanese share prices were far from reflecting the true potential of that market and how we took advantage of this situation.

When I started my career in the capital markets in 1993, the Nikkei 225 index of Japanese shares was in the fourth year of what later turned out to be a long bear market. Already at that time it was down to half its 1989 peak. When we established Vltava Fund in 2004, the Nikkei 225 index, after continuing to decline, was already down to just 30% of its peak.

Not surprisingly, few people talked about it, almost no one followed it, and just about no foreign investors invested in it. Japan was simply a country whose stock prices were only falling and not worthy of anyone's attention. China, whose economy was growing rapidly, was drawing much more attention to itself at the time. Just as in the 1980s there had been talk of Japan's rise, in the first decade of this century there was talk about the rise of China. Japan was seen in many eyes by that time as a country with slow GDP growth, an old and declining population, large debt, often struggling with deflation, and, overall, a country with less long-term potential than, say, China. But it is also true that the Japanese have perhaps the longest life expectancy, a healthy population, an absence of poverty and obesity, low levels of corruption and crime, the best infrastructure of any major country in the world, and a sophisticated, homogeneous, and educated population. Japan is also an advanced country technologically, and Japanese companies have invented and/or successfully commercialized a number of products that have since become almost indispensable to consumers. In his book *The Contest for Japan's Economic Future*, Richard Katz (2024) gives some examples, just to mention a few: the microwave oven for consumers (Sharp), the handheld calculator (Sharp in competition with Texas Instruments), a whole range of computer chips that later became standard (Sharp and Toshiba), the digital watch (Casio and Seiko), the transistor radio (Sony), the VCR video player (Sony and Panasonic), the Triniton color television (Sony), single-lens reflex cameras and later digital cameras (Nikon and Canon), compact discs (Sony), the Walkman (Sony), laptop computers using the same DOS operating system as does a PC (Toshiba), LCD screens (Seiko and Sharp), lithium-ion batteries (Sony and Asahi Kasei), IG networks for mobile phones (NTT), 3G mobile telephones (NTT Docomo), and flexible endoscopes (Olympus).

Japan's Break with the Past

Vltava Fund is a global equity fund and invests in stocks from around the world. Therefore, we were interested in the Japanese market from the outset as a source of potentially attractive investments. The Japanese market is now the second largest in the world by market capitalization after the U.S. market. It was also relatively large 20 years ago, offering investors several thousand listed companies. We made our first investment in Japan in 2005 and several others followed in the years thereafter. We were surprised by how broad and diverse the Japanese stock market is and, in particular, how cheap many of stocks are there. In addition, we have been able to observe several important changes taking place in Japan that could gradually make it more possible to unlock the potential of that market and attract the attention of foreign investors. I will focus here on the two that I believe are most important for investors. The first I would describe as bottom-up changes and the second as top-down changes.

Let's start by thinking about what the following products have in common: cars, televisions, headphones, laptops, smartphones, watches, kitchen appliances, routers, scanners, photography equipment, electric toothbrushes, Tesla batteries, HP printers, Boeing airplanes, and every Apple product. What they have in common is that all have a high content of Japanese components. You could stick a "Japan inside" sticker on every one of them. According to Ulrike Schaede (from whose book *The Business Reinvention of Japan* I draw some information and terms in this text), when you buy an iPhone or other smartphone, a quarter to a third of the content is from Japan (the most of any country). But among Japanese companies we can find, too, others that, while less visible, actually have much more dominant market positions. For example, specialty chemicals necessary for semiconductor production, such as fluorinated polyimide, hydrogen fluoride, and photoresist, are almost monopolistically supplied by Japanese firms JSR and TOK (80–90% global market share). Then there are small electric motors for cars: 80%; carbon fiber: 66%; advanced sensors: 40–70%, depending on type; certain areas of medical and office automation equipment: greater than 70%; and machines and equipment for LCD panel production: up to 90%. These are all global market shares of Japanese companies. A whole range of global manufacturers are heavily dependent on Japanese supplies.

Indeed, without fanfare, quietly, and while not drawing the attention of the broader investment public, a kind of strategic redirection process has been ongoing among Japanese companies over the past two decades. This is something Schaede calls in her book an "aggregate niche strategy." Many firms have found their relatively narrow, and at times perhaps seemingly inconspicuous, market segments and have built strong, often leading positions within them. In aggregate, this completely changes the nature of the Japanese market. Richard Katz contradicts Schaede a little in the sense that, while what she says is true, he thinks that the impact on the overall economy is less than Schaede contends. In my view, this is primarily evidence that the innovative character of Japanese companies, which operated in many sectors during the 1980s and 1990s, and in some cases even in dominant global positions, has not disappeared and must continue to be reckoned with.

Simultaneous with this strategic redirection, a kind of organizational renewal is going on within Japanese firms. Traditional attitudes and values, such as lifetime employment, hierarchies based upon tenure, the status of women, and so forth are gradually being reassessed, and firms are becoming more flexible, innovative, and efficient. In many cases, criticisms of the management style of individual Japanese companies are justified. When we analyzed them over time, we often were bothered by things like low return on capital, low ROE, too much cash idling on the balance sheet, cross-ownership of companies, minimal pressure to create shareholder value, and so on. On the other hand, we found numerous examples of companies that were leaders in their industries and were also well managed. What both groups of companies had in common was that their shares were cheap. Whenever we compared individual Japanese companies with their European or American competitors, their valuations were generally significantly lower. The Japanese market as a whole was also significantly cheaper. For many years, it was one of the most undervalued among the developed markets. At the same time, no one was interested in it. When I went around the world to various investment conferences, no one talked much about Japanese investment opportunities. If someone occasionally spoke up about this, that person was received with polite condescension as someone who had apparently not yet noticed that Japanese stocks were dead and had no potential.

Interest in Japan picked up around 2012 with the advent of so-called Abenomics. This was a name for economic policies pursued by the Liberal Democratic Party (LDP), which led the Japanese government after the December 2012 general election. It was headed by Prime Minister Shinzo Abe, the political program's namesake. Abenomics had several objectives and instruments and combined monetary easing, budgetary stimulus, and structural reforms. If I were to say that Abenomics drew attention to Japan, that attention was focused primarily on the impact of Abenomics on the Japanese economy from a macroeconomic perspective. The stock market itself, however, was still a bit on the sidelines. Indeed, Japanese equities were not a bet on any macroeconomic trends but on deep structural changes in corporate governance that could deliver much higher margins and returns on capital. To understand them and trace their effect in individual Japanese companies was quite difficult.

Investors could not shake the image that they still had in their heads of Japanese companies in the late 20th century. At that time, it was typical that the importance of lifelong employment was emphasized, that seniority of management positions was often determined by age more so than skills, and that individual companies had close relationships with their so-called main banks. Because bankruptcies were not common and both companies and banks tried to avoid them at all costs, the result was the existence of a number of zombie companies that the banks were keeping on life support. Associated with this, too, were frequent and large bank holdings in companies and even greater cross-ownership of companies. Management shareholdings tended to be minimal and many companies and banks were in poor shape. Be that as it may, things were changing. Already in 2002, the Japanese government came up with a financial revitalization program to address the problem of bad bank loans in particular. By 2012, the banks were in incomparably better shape.

In 2014 came further pressure on the efficiency of Japanese companies and the so-called Corporate Governance Code. In the following years, this code has undergone several modifications, the aims being to raise both the level of corporate governance and its effectiveness while also getting management actually to see the creation of shareholder value as one of its priorities. The Tokyo Stock Exchange later added to the pressure on Japanese companies. In 2020, it divided the market into Prime, Standard, and Growth segments, and it was such things as the quality of governance, communication with investors, and efforts to increase shareholder value in the medium and long term that would determine to which segment each stock would be assigned.

The Tokyo Stock Exchange's management brought even more pressure to bear in 2023 when it came up with another measure to increase the efficiency of listed companies. In its project given the name Action on Cost of Capital-Conscious Management and Other Requests, the exchange even required listed companies to implement a series of measures on an ongoing basis. Firms were to start by seeking a proper understanding of their own cost of capital and analyzing their own profitability and balance sheets. They were to continue by preparing and disclosing plans to improve their own efficiency and were to report to investors on the progress of these efforts. Among other things, the stock exchange was concerned that the shares of many Japanese companies were trading below book value (about half of them at the time) and that their businesses were producing low ROEs. If managements did nothing about this and did not present a clear plan to improve the situation, then their companies were at risk of not being able to sustain themselves in the Prime segment of the market and, in the extreme case, of being delisted from the exchange altogether. This threat, together with the efforts of the firms' managements to save face, has and will have positive benefits for their shareholders. From an overall perspective, it is quite unprecedented that an initiative leading to more efficient management of Japanese companies and higher returns on capital has been taken by the stock exchange itself. It has even created the JPX Prime 150 index, which includes companies that must meet two basic conditions: their return on equity (ROE) must be greater than their costs of capital, and their shares must trade above book value. I have not seen anything else like this anywhere in the world. It's a bit early to assess the reaction of Japanese companies and the impact on their share prices, but the first numbers already are coming in. So far, it appears that about half of the companies have increased their dividends, about a quarter of the companies have started buying back their own shares, and about one-eighth have decided to sell their cross holdings and strategic stakes in other companies. Corporate stock prices are reacting most positively to sales of cross shareholdings and share buybacks. Overall, stock prices of firms that have not yet come up with a plan are the poorest performers.

A Simple and Effective Form for Investing in Japanese Equities

Having been involved in the Japanese market as investors since 2005, we have been able to observe the reforms that are taking place there and how the management of individual companies is gradually improving. A more detailed description of the various measures and reforms, whether at the macro or micro level, could be the subject of a separate book and does not belong here. For us, what was important was that the reforms and changes initiated at the turn of the century were gaining momentum and breadth, they were producing discernable results, and the scissors between the potential of Japanese firms and their valuations were becoming more and more open. As late as the middle of the second decade of this century, the Japanese market still stood outside the attention of most investors. We found ourselves in a situation where we had to make a decision about what our future presence in the Japanese market would look like. We realized that we did not have enough capacity at Vltava Fund to cover the Japanese market in sufficient detail alongside the European and North American stock markets. We have long seen North America and Europe as our main areas of focus and did not want to split our resources and move more into Japan to analyze individual local stocks. We therefore considered two alternatives: either not to invest in Japan at all or to invest there through the index in a passive manner. We did not even consider the third option, which would have been to look only superficially at Japanese stocks and buy one here and there when it caught our eye. That would have been amateurish.

It seemed a shame not to invest in Japan at all, because we had accumulated enough knowledge over the previous 10-plus years to find that market attractive. We therefore decided to go with the second option and have held the Nikkei 225 index since 2017. In our otherwise actively managed fund, this is the sole passive investment. Passive investing can be a good form of investing for an investor if it is based on thorough analysis and if it makes sense both in relation to price and composition of the underlying asset. The Nikkei 225 index met both requirements. The only question was how to make a passive investment in Japanese equities. If we took the simplest route and bought an index fund or ETF, there were two significant drawbacks: the full cash outlay and high currency risk. For example, if we wanted to invest $10 million in a Japanese index fund, we would need to buy an ETF for $10 million, and all $10 million would simultaneously be exposed to the currency risk of the underlying asset, the Japanese yen. We regarded currency risk to be substantial in the case of Japan. That concern turned out to be well founded, because at the time we invested in the Nikkei index, the yen/dollar exchange rate was approximately 110. As I write these lines, it is approximately 150. If we had chosen to invest through a fund that hedges currency risk, there would have been hedging costs, which are themselves not insignificant.

We therefore chose a different investment variant, which is to hold the Nikkei 225 index by means of futures contracts. Stock index futures are purely cash-settled contracts based on a stock index. A futures contract is a derivative that commits traders to buy or sell an underlying asset on a specified date at a predetermined price. Index futures are settled daily and traded by futures brokers on stock exchanges. They are used for a number of reasons, including, for example, speculation, hedging, or as part of various trading and investment strategies. We have chosen to use them for long-term index holdings. This approach has its advantages. It does not require the full outlays of cash, as the investor does not buy the entire underlying asset but only commits to settle the difference between the value of the underlying asset when buying the futures and its value when selling the futures. To do this, a fraction of the cash required by the exchange for the so-called initial margin is sufficient. The amount of this guarantee is then adjusted on a daily basis during the holding period of the futures contract according to the developing value of the underlying asset. This is known as the maintenance margin. It can go up or down. With futures, it is possible to achieve the same economic result as through a full cash investment in an index but while utilizing only a fraction of the cash.

A second advantage is that holding futures almost completely eliminates currency risk. The currency risk here is not related to the entire volume of the underlying asset, but only to the unrealized gain (or loss) on the futures contract currently held. It is tiny, without material impact, and essentially completely negligible. It was precisely the ability to avoid currency risk that was critical for us in choosing to go with futures. In practice, the way our investment works is that we always buy the nearest traded quarterly futures contract and roll it forward one quarter each quarter. For example, at the beginning of September, we sell the contract that matures in September, thereby settling in cash the gain or loss made while holding it, and buy the contract that matures in December. We then do the same in December, March, and June. In this way, we hold the Nikkei 225 index for the long term and can easily adjust the size of the position. Another thing to note is that we buy each new contract at a price lower than that for which we sell the old contract. The price of a contract that has just a few days to expire is almost no different from the price of the index to which it is linked. This is logical. However, the price of a futures contract that expires in three months is different from the current price of the index. There must exist what is termed *spot-future* parity. This is the condition that, if an asset can be purchased today and held until the futures contract is realized, then the value of the futures contract should be equal to the current spot price adjusted for the cost of money, dividends, so-called "convenience yield," and any other costs (e.g., storage). Spot-future parity is an application of the law of one price. Because interest costs in Japan have all along been and remain to this day lower than the dividend yield of the index, futures with more distant expiration dates must cost less than do futures with expiration dates closer up. Thus, with every quarterly rollover we reduce the purchase price for those contracts. This has already fallen from an initial level of around 20,000 yen to around 16,000 yen today. This carry benefit will continue so long as short-term interest rates in Japan remain below the dividend yield of stocks in the Nikkei 225 index.

The economic benefit of holding the index through futures is even greater than indicated by the increase in the value of the index and the gradual reduction in our purchase price, due to the dividend yield of the index being higher than are interest rates. In fact, each quarterly rollover brings a cash flow into the fund that is cumulatively highly positive, and this can be invested over time in other stocks held by Vltava Fund. Compound interest here runs at twice the rate.

Over the past 12 years, the Nikkei 225 index has risen by 3.2 times in value. The high-yielding and investor-preferred U.S. market, represented by the S&P 500 index, has risen threefold over the same period. This is a similar return. The difference, however, is that the U.S. index has kept pace with the Japanese index only at the cost of becoming significantly more costly as seen in its substantially rising P/E. Corporate profits in the Nikkei 225 index rose by 3.4 times for the period, while corporate profits in the U.S. S&P 500 index rose by just 1.3 times. The P/E of Japanese stocks in the index is currently about 17× while the P/E for the U.S. index stands today above 28×. Japanese stock prices are rising not primarily because they have become popular but because the profits of the companies there are climbing rapidly. When we add to this the facts that Japanese companies' indebtedness is much lower than that of U.S. companies and that changes in the way Japanese companies are managed and the drive to create shareholder value are far from exhausted, then holding an index of Japanese stocks still strikes us as attractive for the long term. Recently, a variety of advisors and self-proclaimed investment influencers have sprung up like mushrooms on social media. While most of them have never managed money entrusted to them and have no experience of working with real clients, that doesn't stop them from dishing out advice on all sides. Many of them recommend buying the S&P 500 index as the only sound investment strategy. They usually base their advice on the fact that it has worked out great (at least in their opinions) in recent years. When you meet one of these influencers, try to tease them a little and ask why they don't recommend the Japanese index instead of the U.S. index, which has done even better in recent years, is nevertheless still cheaper, and, above all, has much faster corporate earnings growth.

The developments that have taken place in the Japanese corporate sector over the past 20 years are interesting. What is even more intriguing to me is that the low cost of Japanese equities, combined with the major changes underway, has long been on the radar of investors around the world and still has received but minimal attention for many years. Yet, Japan is not some obscure country that no one has heard of. It is the second-largest stock market in the world. When Warren Buffett invested in five leading Japanese trading companies, termed *sogo shosha* (Mitsubishi, Mitsui, Itochu, Marubeni and Sumitomo), on his 90th birthday in 2020, we took it as a confirmation of our view on Japanese equities in general. When Buffett then described how incredibly cheap these stocks were, we knew exactly what he was talking about.

This entire chapter provides another example of how an active approach to investing can pay off and how one can find value even in big markets. At the same time, it is an example of how the difference between price and value can be exploited in various ways. This might be achieved even by investing in an index if a suitable form for doing so presents itself and if the investment has an attractive combination of risk and return. I have seen several situations in my lifetime where a country's entire stock market can be considered a hidden investment treasure. It is almost certain that such opportunities will continue to occur in the future.

Chapter 10

Oil

Seeking Treasure in a Sector That Is Out of Favor

Chapter 9 was about finding value from a macro perspective in one region or a single country. This chapter, too, will take a macro perspective, but it will be about one particular global industry: oil and gas production. I'll focus on some neglected or misunderstood realities about how the world works and its investment implications. I am aware that this chapter stands out thematically from the rest of the book, but I decided in the end to include it as written. The next chapter builds directly upon this one, which was the first reason to include it. The second reason is that issues relating to energy and its production and consumption directly or indirectly affect almost every other sector and should be taken into account by investors.

Let me start by posing a question for you to contemplate. Think about the poorest country you've ever visited. As for me, I would nominate

Lesotho, for example, or some remote parts of Tibet. Why do this? I ask because I think that if one remembers how poor many parts of the world are compared to the part you or I live in, then one can better comprehend the content of this chapter.

Some Alarming Statistics

Let's start by looking at two sets of facts. The first is the ranking of the world's most populous countries, as shown in Figure 10.1.

Nothing much is surprising here. It is worth noting, though, that only three of these countries can be regarded as rich: the United States, Japan, and Germany. The rest are middle-income to low-income countries. The second set of facts consists in the per capita annual energy consumption (in gigajoules, GJ) in some selected countries and a political unit (Figure 10.2).

At first glance, we are perhaps struck by the huge differences. Each person in the United States consumes on average almost 300 GJ of energy (of all types) per year. In Japan and the EU, it is only 150 GJ, in China about 90 GJ, in Brazil 60 GJ, in India 20 GJ, in Nigeria 5 GJ, and in Ethiopia 2 GJ. The average American, for example, consumes as much energy per day as the average Ethiopian consumes in five months. Multiplying the per capita energy consumption by the population shows the total annual energy consumption of these countries (Figure 10.3).

You can see from these figures, for example, that although Japan and Ethiopia have similar populations, Japan has 70 times the energy consumption. Also, Brazil and Nigeria, for instance, have similar populations, but Brazil's energy consumption is 11 times that of Nigeria's. The United States consumes 3.5 times the energy as does India, which has more than 4 times the population, and so on. Now imagine that people in poor and middle-income countries have ambitions to live a better life and gradually approach the standard of living we are accustomed to in our countries, for example. These ambitions are natural and logical, and we must cheer them on. Achieving them, however, will entail much greater demands for energy consumption. Figure 10.4 suggests just how huge these demands can be.

If, for example, China were to reach the same standard of living as the EU in terms of energy consumption, then this would mean additional energy consumption close to that of the United States today. If India wanted

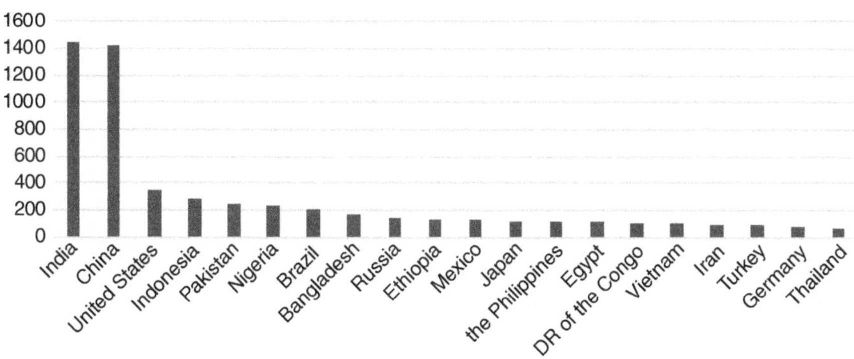

Figure 10.1 The world's most populous countries (mil).
Source: Worldometer.

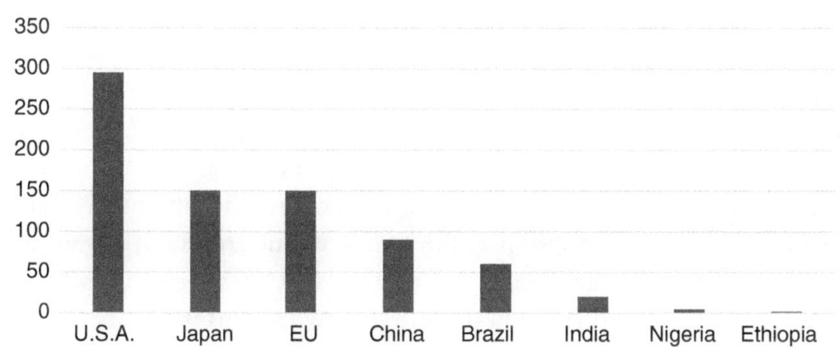

Figure 10.2 Annual energy consumption per capita in gigajoules (GJ).
Source: Vltava Fund.

	GJ/capita	Inhabitants (mil)	Consumption
USA	295	345	101,775
Japan	150	123	18,450
EU	150	450	67,500
China	90	1419	127,710
Brazil	60	211	12,660
India	20	1450	29,000
Nigeria	5	232	1,160
Ethiopia	2	132	264

Figure 10.3 Total annual energy consumption.

Ambition	Increase	Equivalent
China to EU	85,140	Nearly another USA
Brazil to China	6,330	5× Nigeria
India to Brazil	58,000	Nearly another EU
Nigeria to India	3,480	Four times
Ethiopia to India	2,376	Ten times

Figure 10.4   Potential growth in energy consumption.

to catch up with Brazil, it would require an increase in energy consumption of almost as much as the EU consumes today. For Nigeria to catch up with a still relatively energy-poor India today, it would have to quadruple its energy consumption. I am aware that these are only rough figures, but they are huge in any case. OPEC, in its *2023 World Oil Outlook 2045*, states that it expects global energy demand to increase by 23% by 2045 and that this will require more than $14 trillion of investment ($610 billion per year). The actual increase in demand may be even greater, as the OPEC analysis has apparently not taken sufficiently into account the potentially huge increase in energy consumption in the richest countries resulting from the construction of data centers, and it has assumed that energy consumption in the richer OECD countries will decline somewhat. This now seems quite unlikely. Investors often talk about AI as the industry of the future and the oil and gas sector as a relic of the past. But the former cannot exist without the latter and certainly not to the extent required.

The Likely Increase in Demand Is Frightening

Vltava Fund's portfolio also includes shares of the Canadian company Brookfield Corporation. Its CEO, Bruce Flatt, writes regular letters to shareholders. In his letter for the second quarter of 2024, he also discusses the expected increase in global energy consumption. His numbers are literally breathtaking. Flatt states:

> The next 20 years will be an unprecedented period for electricity build-out. The electrification of industrial capacity, automobiles, heating for houses, and other uses is driving unprecedented growth in the demand for

electricity. On top of that, the world is adding data centers for AI and cloud computing at a stunning pace.

To put this in perspective, the global installed capacity for electricity is approximately 8,000 gigawatts. To meet expected demand, this installed capacity will need to expand to more than 20,000 gigawatts in the next 20 years. In addition, nearly half of what exists today will need to be retired, as it is very carbon-intensive. Said differently, we need to more than double the current capacity (which was largely built over the past 50 years) while also replacing approximately 50% of what we have. Nothing like this has ever been attempted, but it is essential in order to reach the world's net-zero goals and drive the AI revolution.

The increase in demand for power to run data centers used in computing capacity for AI is only starting to be understood and is largely excluded in the above calculations. The computing capacity required for algorithms to advance medical discovery and industrial productivity is large. The amount needed to power computing capacity to train robotics towards intelligence nearer to humans is vast. But, when we reach that goal, productivity advances in many businesses will be very significant.

Our recent agreement with Microsoft was a landmark deal in corporate power contracting. At over 10.5 gigawatts, it is nearly eight times larger than any other deal ever signed. But, for perspective, this is just 10.5 of the more than 16,000 gigawatts required in the next 20 years. This is a $10 billion plus deal, which indicates the scale of the total capital required to meet power demand and decarbonize – hundreds of trillions.

If Flatt's numbers are in fact close to what will actually need to be built and how much energy consumption will increase, then maximum use of all possible energy sources and huge investments will be required. In addition, energy prices are likely to rise and have an inflationary effect.

Looking at the world in terms of energy need, consumption, and production offers a number of surprising and on the whole not encouraging data points. Today, there are about 8.1 billion people on Earth. It is estimated that about 600 million of them have no electricity at all and that some 3 billion suffer from chronic energy shortages of all kinds. Three billion of the planet's inhabitants today have per capita energy consumption roughly equivalent to that of Germany and France in 1860. Globally, Africa ranks lowest for the standard of living of its people, highest in the rankings showing chronic shortages in energy consumption, and highest in terms of population growth. Over the next few decades, more than half of new births are expected to come from Africa and the Middle East.

The world today faces chronic shortages in energy production. Future global energy demand will be driven primarily by a striving to raise the living standards of the world's 5 billion poor people. Their additional energy demands will far exceed any expected savings among the rich countries. This situation is exacerbated by the fact that the resources needed for energy production are not evenly distributed across the globe. Some regions have surpluses (the United States, Canada, Russia, Australia, Norway, Brazil, Argentina, etc.), while others have shortages (Africa in the first place).

Relationship Between Energy Consumption, Energy Availability, and Population Wealth

There exist many statistical studies examining the relationship between GDP per capita and energy consumption in the various countries. Figure 10.5 shows that there is a relatively close relationship between these variables.

The richer the country, the greater the energy consumption. This is to be expected, of course. But the question is what is the cause and effect? At first glance, one might say that people's greater wealth allows them to consume more energy. But what if the causality is reversed? What if countries are richer because they have widespread access to large amounts of cheap energy? This argument would be suggested by the rise in the standard of living of the world's major countries over the past few centuries. The standard of living in the most developed countries of the world did not begin to rise steeply until sometime around 1800. First and fastest, it was in countries where energy was widely available and accessible in increasingly advanced forms. The author Václav Smil even directly takes the view in his books that the basis for the growth in wealth of society and the development of humankind is an abundance of low-cost energy. Thus, if we want the poor two-thirds of the planet's population to gradually fulfill their desire for a better standard of living, then the world urgently needs every bit of energy it can produce.

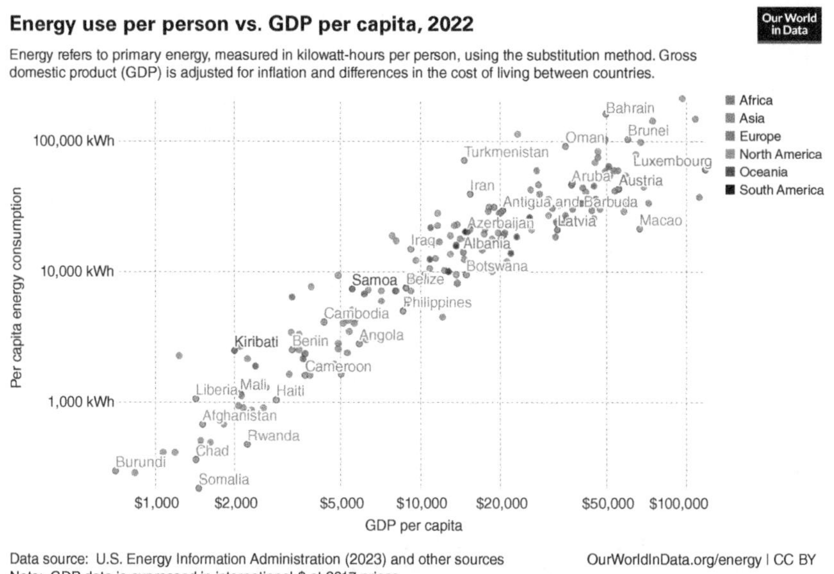

Figure 10.5 GDP per capita versus energy consumption per capita. *Source:* U.S. Energy Information Administration / CC BY 4.0.

According to Smil, the great push to replace fossil fuels rapidly with renewable sources that we are witnessing can succeed only at the cost of lowering the living standards of people in rich countries and denying people in poor countries their aspirations for a significantly better standard of living. Many of us who live in the rich countries of the West might say that there is nothing wrong with lowering our own standard of living. I would readily agree with that. But do we in the rich West have the right to negatively influence the living standards of the poor five billion? Can this be considered humane and morally right? There is no easy answer to that.

If the living standards of the poor and middle-income countries are to rise, huge investments will be needed in areas that are wholly commonplace. In his book *How the World Really Works*, Smil argues that civilization and its development stand on four basic pillars. These are not artificial intelligence, nanotechnology, 5G, or the quest to conquer Mars. They are ammonia, steel, cement, and plastics. Without the artificial production of ammonia through Haber-Bosch synthesis and the fertilizers it is used to produce, it would be impossible to produce enough food for eight billion people. Without steel and cement, it is impossible to build what is needed, and plastics are such an important part of almost every aspect of life that we often do not even realize it. We find them in the packaging industry, the automotive industry, electronics, construction, furniture, clothing, and footwear. Plastics are also widely used today in modern medicine, sports, and toys. They are well suited to use in agriculture and horticulture, fencing and tools, and so forth. Try to go a day in your life without using anything that contains plastic or is made with plastic. Basically, it's impossible. That's the reality.

Ammonia, steel, cement, and plastics all have a few more common denominators. There are no adequate substitutes for them, their production is extremely energy intensive, and production cannot be achieved without fossil fuels. Even the transition to renewables is hugely energy intensive and cannot be done without fossil fuels. Just think about how many kilograms of nonferrous metals (lithium, cobalt, copper, nickel), graphite, steel, and plastics are contained in one electric car battery. Metal mining and processing are also highly energy intensive and are not possible without using fossil fuels. The same is true for the construction of wind power plants. Each wind turbine requires large amounts of cement, steel, and plastics and is built using heavy equipment that runs on diesel.

There is a great contradiction between what the world needs to grow and develop and the transition toward a greater proportion of renewables joined with pressure to reduce the extraction and use of fossil fuels as quickly as possible. When we look specifically at the oil and gas sector, which is the main focus of this chapter, the pressure is enormous. Extraction companies are being shamed and their managements pilloried. Sometimes even their shareholders themselves are pushing the companies to curb production. Banks refuse to finance them, insurance companies refuse to insure them, and investors, if they invest in their shares, often become the target of attacks from outside. However, civilization is unable to survive without the use of fossil fuels (especially oil and gas), let alone develop further. This would require additional massive investment into the development of further extraction.

At this point, I want to emphasize one important point. This chapter is not intended to be, and therefore should not be seen as, sociopolitical agitation. I am not clever enough to lecture the world on what it should look like, and I have no ambition in this regard. It is quite enough for me if I can guess which direction the world will take. I always remind myself that it is not investors' job to project into their investments what they would like to happen or what would please them. Investors should project what they think will happen. What one wishes for and what one thinks will happen are two different things. What happens in the world is not dependent upon what each of us as individuals wishes for. It is not easy to guess where the world will go, but a simple observation of the world around us can tell us a lot.

Is the Market Wrong in Estimating Future Oil Prices?

Back to the oil and gas sector. The situation I have described, that is to say, the great discrepancy between the expected increase in energy consumption, driven primarily by the desire for a better life for the five billion poor people, and the desire to limit oil and gas production has several major investment implications. In my estimation, demand for oil itself will continue to rise. From its current (record) level of around 103 million barrels per day, it should reach somewhere in the region of 116 million barrels per day over the next 20 years. It will continue to rise even though renewables will constitute a much greater share of the overall energy mix than they do today. Indeed, the overall growth in world energy consumption will be so large that it will take an absolute increase in oil and gas consumption to cover it. For the supply side (i.e., the oil-producing companies) to meet this growing demand, we estimate that more than $500 billion a year would need to be invested in development and production growth alone (plus an additional $100 billion annually in oil processing and transportation). Today and in recent years, global investment in oil development and growth is much less, somewhere between $300 billion and $400 billion per year. Investment last reached $500 billion in 2014. This is largely because the social environment for oil production is quite hostile, and the management of oil companies do not want to spend billions and billions on investments with a view many years into the future while taking on risks and making their lives difficult. Thanks to low investment, the oil companies have high free cash flow and prefer to return money to their shareholders. The likely result is a long-term supply-side deficit in oil production with a negative impact on society in general in the form of high oil prices. In the long term, the longer efforts to curb oil production persist, the higher the oil price will be. Those who will be hurt most will be ordinary people and, above all, poorer countries.

If the mood in society were reversed, investment in oil and gas development and production growth would be given the green light, the price of oil would be lower in the long term with all its positive effects on consumers, but, paradoxically, the shareholders of the production companies could be expected to be worse off. Higher investment in extraction would mean much lower free cash flow for oil companies, more risk, and more frequent managerial mistakes. In such an environment, it might be better to prefer investing into shares of companies providing capital goods and services to the extraction sector rather than shares of the oil companies themselves. It is more likely, however, that we will continue to live in an environment that is hostile to oil and gas investment, with the amount of investment being insufficient and the price of oil unnecessarily high.

Another important investment implication, then, will be that whichever of the two alternatives described is closer to reality, a major competitive advantage will be enjoyed by those companies and countries that have lower-cost sources of energy and that always have energy available in the quantities needed. This competitive advantage (and disadvantage) increasingly has been reflected in recent years in the performance of companies in different parts of the world and in the economic growth of individual countries.

There are many conflicting opinions in the oil market. Much of the rich West can easily succumb to the impression that crude oil will not be needed much in the future. But the world is not California and Germany. The world is more like China, India, Africa, and Latin America. The world, above all, is five billion poor people with their desire for a better life. This cannot be ignored, and this is where most of the growth in oil consumption will come from. In their imaginations, some people paint a world in which there will be no need for fossil fuels, including the most important of them all, oil. They would like to get as close to this ideal as possible. However, this view ignores how the world actually works, what it needs, and what it cannot do without. Moreover, calling for a halt to investment in oil extraction could lead to energy and economic chaos. In contrast, we have the unpleasant facts of chronic energy shortages in the world today, enormous expected growth in energy consumption in coming years, and an insufficiency of investment in energy production, or in the case of oil, in its extraction.

Everyone can ponder for themselves what this will mean. Our analyses lead us to conclude that all this points to a long-term trend for the price of oil to be higher rather than lower due to an excess of demand over supply. I would very much like to see the oil price as low as possible in the long term. This would have a positive impact on the middle- and lower-income populations. Unfortunately, the trend so far is in exactly the opposite direction. (By the way, I come to the same conclusion for other commodities, like copper, for example. But the copper market is incomparably smaller than is the oil market. Unlike a high oil price, a high copper price will have only limited impact on the economy and consumers.)

How We Can Take Advantage of This

What can investors do if they conclude that the oil price will be higher in the long run than anticipated by the main analytical consensus and also higher than the oil market is currently indicating? When investing, it is usually best to express an opinion in the simplest and most direct investment possible. If you think oil is too cheap, buy oil. How can this be done? The oil market is huge and liquid. The most efficient way for a financial investor to invest in and trade oil is through futures. The principle of oil futures is similar to that of index futures, the difference being that when oil futures are held until expiration of the contract, there is physical settlement of the commodity. This means that the holder is obliged to take delivery of the oil: 1,000 barrels for each contract. Only a small fraction of contracts are settled in this manner, however. The vast majority of them are sold before they mature. This is also the only possible settlement route enabled by brokerage firms for retail investors. They either force you to sell the contract before it expires or roll it into a later maturity. The best way to gain direct exposure to the oil market is through West Texas Intermediate (WTI) light sweet crude oil futures traded on the Chicago Mercantile Exchange (CME). It is the most liquid and widely followed crude oil contract in the world. Monthly maturities are available for 10 years into the future. If we plot the current futures prices for each maturity on a graph, we get what is termed a forward curve. Its shape can tell us a lot about how the market feels about future oil prices. Forward curves can take many shapes showing changes in value at different time points along the curve. The two most typical shapes are called *contango* and *backwardation*. See Figure 10.6.

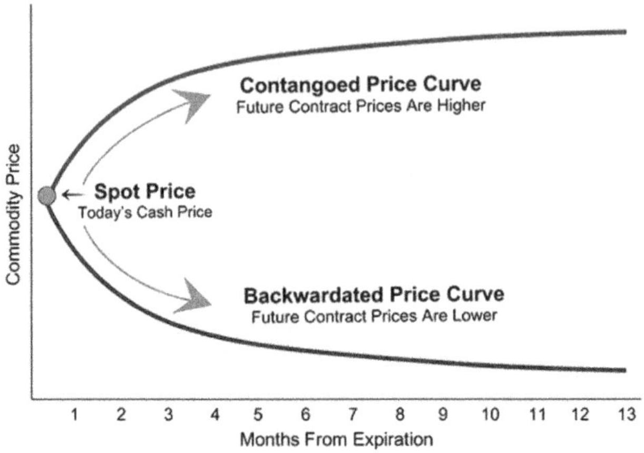

Figure 10.6   Forward oil price curve.

When the market is in contango (unfortunately, English does not have a better word for this), futures contracts trade at a gradually increasing premium to the spot price. Physically delivered futures contracts may be in contango due to fundamental factors such as costs of storage, financing, transportation, and insurance. Futures prices may change over time as market participants change their views on the future expected spot price; the forward curve thus changes and may move from contango to backwardation.

If the spot price is higher than future prices, and these create a downward sloping – or inverted – forward curve, we say that the market is in backwardation. The forward curve of futures may become backwardated for contracts for which physical delivery is possible because ownership of the physical commodity may be advantageous, for example, to keep the production process going. This is called the *convenience yield*, and it is an implied return on holding inventory. The convenience yield is inversely proportional to the level of inventory. When inventories are high, the convenience yield is low, and when inventories are low, the yield is high. Over time, as the futures contract approaches maturity, the futures price converges to the spot price; otherwise, there would be an arbitrage opportunity. This process is termed *convergence*. With the typical shape of the curve, whether in backwardation or contango, convergence for distant maturities runs slowly at first and gradually accelerates. It tends to be fastest in the last few months before contract maturity.

Currently, the forward curve is in the shape of backwardation. The spot price of $68 is the highest and prices are gradually declining as maturities lengthen. There are many and diverse financial and economic theories concerning the shapes of forward curves. To simplify, the shape of the curve is influenced by fundamental reasons as well as by structural or technical reasons. The fundamental view is based on estimates of future demand and supply and seeks to predict which future price will bring the two sides of the market into equilibrium. Structural and technical reasons are related to financial flows in the oil market. The question of whether the price of oil is influenced more by fundamentals or by cash flows has always been part of the oil market. For us as investors, the interesting time point will be when both fundamental and technical factors act in the same direction on the oil price and create an investment opportunity. If most market players are expecting weakening demand for oil and at the same time there is an abundance of oil on the supply side, then it is logical that they envision a gradually declining oil price and a forward curve in backwardation. Money flows in the oil market also tend to push the forward curve into backwardation. Oil producers use financial markets to hedge against a drop in the oil price. Often they sell part of their future production, thereby pushing the more distant points on the forward curve below the current spot price. There are more sellers trying to hedge against a possible future decline in the oil price than there are buyers trying to hedge against a possible rise. The main buyers are airlines and refiners, but their volumes are much smaller compared to those of oil producers. Oil producers also have a much greater incentive to hedge against unacceptable developments in oil prices than do consumers. The concept of normal backwardation was introduced by the British economist John Maynard Keynes. He described it as a situation where the futures price for a particular expiry month is lower than the expected spot price for that month. He argued that producers seeking to hedge pay a risk premium to speculators, which leads to normal backwardation.

If an investor reaches the conclusion that oil's current spot price is too low from a fundamental perspective (how to estimate the long-term price of oil is in the next chapter) and that the shape of the forward curve is still in significant backwardation due to fundamental and technical reasons, one can take advantage of this by buying futures with more distant maturities and holding them until almost maturity. One can thus benefit simultaneously from both gradual assertion of the fundamentals one expects and the progressive convergence caused by technical and structural factors. This is exactly the approach we at Vltava Fund would take if we were investing directly in commodities. We would seek to express our view on the future price of oil through various combinations of contracts with different maturities, holding periods, and possibly in combination with options on futures. As we are an equity fund, however, we must apply our view of the oil market through investing in equities. There are countless ways to do this. We will describe one of them in the next chapter.

Chapter 11

Cenovus Energy

Seeking Treasure in a Sector That Is Out of Favor, Part II

The previous two chapters deviated from the text up to that point inasmuch as they did not relate to investing in a particular, single stock (i.e., taking a bottom-up view) but instead attempted to find value by looking at a macro view from above, which may be termed a top-down approach. In the remaining chapters, I will return to the search for value in individual stocks. The first of these will be from the oil and gas exploration and production sector and thereby will be directly related to the previous chapter. This sector is largely not of interest to passive investors and therefore lies outside the mainstream of money flows. The oil and gas industry's share of the S&P 500 index is only about 4%. This is much less than Apple's share alone, for instance, and the industry's profits are also greater than Apple's. What is also quite different between the two is that oil and gas are indispensable. If Apple and all its products were to disappear from the world tomorrow, that would be a shame, but life would go on virtually unabated. If the oil and gas companies were to disappear tomorrow along with their production, however, the world would collapse.

The question nevertheless remains whether there are good investment opportunities among the oil producers. In our opinion, yes, there are. That said, it did take us quite a while to convince ourselves of that. Between 2005 and 2008, we at Vltava Fund were quite active in this sector with our investments. We had analyzed several dozen companies from all over the world, ranging from small, so-called "junior oil companies" that are not yet producing oil to the largest supermajors and national oil companies. At that time, the market environment was playing into the hands of oil producers. The price of oil was rising, and there was talk of a new era of globalization and China's rise. After the big drop in oil prices in 2008, however, we left the industry altogether. This was not because of the low oil price. It was obvious that prices were not going to remain low forever, and because low oil prices usually pull down share prices for the oil producers, this might have been a good time to buy oil and gas stocks at bargain prices. Our main reason related to the behavior of most companies' managements, who preferred risky investments, megalomaniacal acquisitions, and vested interests while often putting the interests of shareholders on the back burner. Two famous quotes from Mark Twain no longer struck us as mere hyperbole. Twain was known to say "A mine is a hole in the ground with a liar on top" and "As for commodities, the only consistently profitable extractive industry is dentistry." A fairly good and detailed knowledge of the industry led us to conclude that it was best to avoid it entirely – at least until the behavior of companies' management would change. We didn't have much faith that such altered behavior was to be expected. Nevertheless, we returned here as investors in 2022 and have held shares of the Canadian company Cenovus Energy in our portfolio ever since.

The main reason for our change of heart was just such a shift in corporate management's behavior and their approach to asset allocation. Previously, management of exploration and production companies had favored absolute growth. They overinvested into new extraction capacity both organically and through numerous acquisitions. They sought to grab as much market share as possible, operated with excessive debt, and were willing to take large long-term risks. The combination of these factors resulted in relatively low free cash flow that could be directed to shareholders. In addition, high debt and long-term investment returns made oil companies vulnerable and susceptible to the cyclical fluctuations for which oil and gas production are well-known. We did not want to invest in such an environment.

Sometime around 2014, however, the attitude and behavior of oil companies' management began to change. In the previous chapter, I mentioned that the last year when the level of investment in oil and gas development reached the $500 billion needed for supply to keep up with demand over the long term was 2014. At that time, the oil price was firmly above $100 per barrel and provided sufficient incentive for investment. In the following two years, however, the oil price fell and it didn't pay for oil companies to invest as much in production. Lingering overcapacity from the pre-2008 oil boom played a role here. The natural reaction of a large part of the oil companies' management was to significantly reduce investment in new production. However, these investments did not return to their original or necessary levels even when the oil price started to rise again in the following years (2020 was a short-term anomaly in terms of the oil price caused by the pandemic). As I described in the previous chapter, I consider the main reason to be that the social environment is quite hostile to oil production, and oil company executives do not want to spend huge sums on investments with a view to many years ahead, take risks, and complicate their lives in these conditions. This situation is pushing the price of oil upward and will continue to do so. Meanwhile, it is accompanied by certain positive developments from the viewpoint of the production companies' shareholders. For many oil companies, we are seeing a shift away from the frantic pursuit of growth with its negative impacts on shareholder value to a much more rational asset allocation and an emphasis on shareholder value creation. We see a restraint in taking risky and long-term investments, fewer large acquisitions, more moderate debt management, and an emphasis on returning excess free cash flow to shareholders. There has been a significant paradigm shift in combination with attractive valuations across the sector that is compounded by near-perfect ignorance on the part of passive investors. This gave rise to sufficient impetus for us to invest in the sector again.

How did we go about stock selection? Valuing shares in an oil and gas company is based upon the same principle as valuing shares in any other sector. The value of the company is equal to the net present value of all future cash flows that shareholders can take home each year without the company's business suffering in its current size and form. However, the extractive sector has some important specifics. All oil companies are in the position of so-called "price takers." This means that they have no influence on the price of oil and gas. The prices of these commodities are also characterized by significant cyclicality. Oil and gas extraction is a highly capital-intensive activity, the investments have long payback periods, the return of the invested amounts itself bears considerable uncertainty, and these investments commonly entail using large amounts of debt. The whole sector is heavily regulated and is also subject to many adverse social pressures.

Nature of the Oil Market

The alpha and omega of oil and gas production companies' valuations is the oil price. There are typically big swings up and down, the main reason being low price elasticity on both the supply and demand sides. Low elasticity means that demand and supply change little and only slowly when the oil price changes. Because oil storage capacity is relatively small in global terms compared to the volume of oil production, even a small imbalance between supply and demand for oil results in large price movements. The low elasticity of demand for oil is mainly because oil has few substitutes. Even if its price falls or rises substantially, people's consumption of goods and services that require oil changes little – especially in the short term, meaning within days or even months. The exact elasticity of demand is difficult to measure, but estimates of its magnitude are somewhere around −0.06. This means that a 10% movement in the price of oil will produce only a 0.6% change in demand in the short term. In the long run (i.e., over a period of years or more), the elasticity is greater because substitutes can be found over time (when the price rises) or, conversely, oil can be substituted for other products (when the price falls). Even in the long run, however, the elasticity of demand for oil remains relatively low and has been estimated at between −0.2 and −0.3.

Moreover, changes (mainly growth) in GDP and personal income have long-term impacts on oil demand. This elasticity can also be estimated and estimates hover around 1. This means that a real increase in personal income of 10% would also lead to a 10% increase in oil demand. For developed countries, this elasticity is estimated at 0.55, and for fast-growing emerging countries, it is estimated at 1.1. As we saw in the previous chapter, the majority of the planet's population can be classified as middle- and low-income countries with ambitions to grow rapidly. With the expected rapid growth in the population's incomes, this part of the world will play the most important role in future oil demand.

And what is the situation for oil and its price on the supply side? Here, too, low price elasticities can be observed. This elasticity is estimated at 0.04 in the short term and 0.35 in the long term. This is because the reaction time to changes in the price of oil in terms of its production is long. If the price of oil rises, the incentive for companies to produce more of it also increases, but they have limited ability to boost production quickly. There is usually little unutilized production capacity in the market that can be activated quickly and without much cost, and, if the oil price rises significantly, even this capacity can quickly be exhausted. Further production growth would be possible only at the cost of investment into new capacities. These capacities, however, are costly, and, above all, it takes a long time – normally several years – to convert the initial investment into a materially significant volume of production.

If the oil price declines, oil companies will limit investment into new capacity, but they will not to any great extent resort to closing down existing capacity. This is because oil production cannot be switched off and on like a light switch. To shut down is costly and economically disadvantageous. The geology of the extraction site also plays a role. In many cases, production simply cannot be interrupted without reducing the recoverability of reserves. That is why we commonly see production companies resorting to curbing production only when the oil price falls below the operating costs of production. For example, when the price of oil fell from over $100 per barrel in 2014 to about one-third of that in 2016, huge amounts of extracted oil were still flooding into the market and the supply side took longer to adjust to the new prices.

The ability of the supply side to respond to rising demand is conditioned upon several factors. First, the management of production companies must become convinced that the price of oil in the long term will be sufficiently high to induce them to invest into new production capacity. Second, they must have the capital needed to make these investments and must be willing to take on the investment risk while knowing that investment cycles and returns in this sector are long. Third, the current level of production is being steadily reduced by the gradual depletion of existing resources. This depletion rate is estimated at 4–8% per annum. If investment into new production capacity were to cease completely, the current level of oil production would fall by more than half within 20 years. This means that much of the investment into new production capacity is only replacing that which is being depleted and not increasing overall output. Replacing depleted capacity is becoming ever more challenging. It will be difficult to repeat the good fortune of the past 15 years, when production, particularly in the United States, has increased significantly as a result of advances in the recoverability of shale oil. Supply, like demand, will eventually find a way to adjust to a possible higher oil price, but this will happen only many years down the line.

The life and investment cycle of a typical extractive resource is long, and in the initial few years it generates a highly negative cash flow for the producing company (investor). First comes the exploration phase. This can take several years. During this phase, the company must obtain a mining or drilling license and carry out a seismic survey of the deposit. If the exploration looks promising, exploratory wells will be drilled, the characteristics of the deposit will be tested, and estimates of the economics of production will be refined. Then comes the appraisal phase, which looks to prove or disprove the commercial appeal of the deposit. This phase is much more costly than is the exploration phase, but the main costs and investments come only in the third phase, termed the development phase. If the appraisal phase proves the resource to be commercially attractive, it is only then that the main investments must be made into the actual extraction, into preparation of the extraction processes, and into the accompanying infrastructure. It is only at the end of this phase that the first production occurs, and, if everything works as expected and the commodity price is favorable, then the cash flow swings from negative to positive. At this point, we could be 5, 7, or even 10 years down the road from the start of the exploration phase. In that time, the extraction company has incurred high operating costs and has invested a large amount of capital into the project. In the next phase, production, it will hope to achieve a return that not only covers the operating costs of extraction but also recovers the costs incurred before extraction and provides a sufficient return on the capital that has been invested into the deposit before and during production. It has a limited time to achieve this, because each

deposit has a finite life and each also faces its own depletion rate. In addition, the company still has to set aside funds for post-extraction site and
environmental reclamation. (Incidentally, the biggest financial beneficiary
of extraction is the state. It needn't incur any extraction costs and needn't
invest any capital into its development. The state just collects taxes and
royalties during extraction.)

Incentive Price

In looking at the main factors that influence the price of oil, it can be said
that in the **short term the price of oil is determined by demand,
but in the long term the price is determined by supply**. In the long
term, the price of oil must be high enough to motivate companies to
make investments sufficiently large to achieve a level of production that
meets demand. We are talking here about the so-called incentive price.
When we analyze a gas and oil company and try to estimate its future free
cash flow, the most important input factor is precisely the estimated future
oil price. It is the price to which the profits of the production companies
are most sensitive. It makes a huge difference whether an oil company sells
oil at $30, $70, $100, or $130 per barrel. At the lower end of that range,
most oil companies will not be able to survive; at the upper end, they will
make fat profits. So, we are attentive to the incentive price estimate.

This estimation is a laborious process wherein one must take into
account a number of factors and often while working with imprecise and
incomplete data. The main inputs we use to estimate the incentive price
are the current level of production and its depletion rate, the cost curve
of the production companies, the capital intensity of the investment
needed to build new production capacity, the required rate of return on
investment, inflation, and the expected level of demand. We are not looking for averages of these indicators for the industry as a whole. Rather,
we are trying to determine how high the incentive price must be to
produce a marginal barrel that exactly balances supply and demand. The
fact that the cost curve for production from more economically viable
sources in the Middle East or Eurasia is around $40 does have an impact
on the oil market, but what matters is where the cost curve will be for
those sources that produce the last barrel required by demand. That is
much higher, and we estimate that it is at or above $80 per barrel.

Moreover, the entire cost curve is being pushed further up by inflation, geopolitical risks, and political obstacles to investment. It is not enough for companies investing into new production capacity to cover their extraction costs. They also need to achieve the required sufficiently high return on capital, and they will insist that all be the greater when geopolitical risk is higher and more obstacles are put in the way of production companies by opponents of oil production.

In summary, then, the main features of the oil and gas extraction industry are that all producers are price takers, the highly cyclical nature of the main commodity price, long investment cycles, working with large amounts of debt, regulatory pressure and interference, and frequent errors by management in asset allocation. Therefore, when selecting oil companies as potential investments, we prefer companies that have immediate high free cash flow, low debt, long-term existing oil reserves, low operating costs and relatively low capital intensity, efficient capital allocation, and operations in stable jurisdictions. There are many oil companies in the world, and we use an exclusionary approach to select them while considering the criteria discussed.

Why We Chose Cenovus Energy

We categorize exploration and production companies into several main groups. The first group consists of the national oil companies (NOCs). These include Saudi Aramco (Saudi Arabia), KPC (Kuwait), NIOC (Iran), CNPC (China), ADNOC (UAE), and Pemex (Mexico). They are quite large. This group produces about 25 million barrels of oil a day. Saudi Aramco alone produces about one-tenth of the world's oil. Most of these companies stand outside the investment realm because they are private. An exception is Saudi Aramco, a small portion of whose shares are traded on the stock exchange, but we would not be interested in making an investment there. The second group consists of the so-called supermajors. These are also sometimes called international oil companies (IOCs). They include Rosneft, Shell, Chevron, TotalEnergies, Marathon Petroleum, ExxonMobil, BP, ENI, and Petrobras. Together, they produce almost as much oil as do the NOCs. Their shares are traded on stock exchanges, but we prefer to avoid them. Because of their market positions, they are subject to the greatest criticism and pressure from politicians and often even from their shareholders themselves. Sometimes it seems to us that they are not even properly aware of their main objective and that their priorities are not firmly established. Their size is also an obstacle to further growth, and they have relatively high costs for discovering and developing new resources. At the other end of the spectrum of production companies are the junior oil companies. These form a third and rather large group, and we avoid them, too. These are younger companies that are either not yet producing or are dependent on a key, and not large, source of production. They are small both in terms of the size of their production and their market capitalizations. Although investing in them can sometimes yield high returns, doing so is too risky and involves a large speculative element. We have no interest in such investments. So, if we exclude all of this, plus production companies where their businesses are centered in jurisdictions that are too risky and unstable, then what is actually available to us that would meet our selection criteria?

It's not much, but it is sufficient for purposes of our investments. For example, several companies in the United States (EOG Resources, Occidental Petroleum, Marathon Oil) and several companies in Canada (Suncor, CNQ, Cenovus) have cleared our screening requirements. Of these, we selected for Vltava Fund's portfolio the Canadian company Cenovus Energy (CVE). It is relatively large (daily production of around 800,000 barrels + refining capacity of 720,000 barrels per day) and has a market capitalization of CAD 42 billion and proven and probable reserves of 8.7 billion barrels of oil equivalent (BBOE), which would be sufficient to produce oil at current levels for 31 years. (Note: This period, measured in years and known as the "reserves life index," is calculated as the total reserves divided by the total annual production.) The company is highly profitable, with immediate high free cash flow, low debt, and low operating costs of production. Because most of the production comes from oil sands, it also has low discovery and exploration costs. New production capacity can be built incrementally and efficiently on a block-by-block basis using the so-called *in situ* production method bearing much less risk than does building production capacity from many conventional sources. Cenovus has an efficient allocation of capital and operates in one of the most stable, albeit not always entirely predictable, jurisdictions.

When it comes to oil production, simply having a resource and knowing how to extract it isn't enough. It is also important to be able to process the oil and transport it to customers. Cenovus has most of its reserves in the Canadian province of Alberta. It is well connected by pipelines both to the large U.S. oil market and to overseas export terminals on the Pacific coast. Cenovus also owns several refineries in both Canada and the United States and is able to process some of its own production there. This is a great advantage, because there exists a large variety of crude oil types and not every refinery can process them. CVE's integrated business model has significant added value.

How expensive are CVE shares? The most important indicator for valuing CVE shares is free cash flow. This is because a production company needs to reinvest a significant portion of its net profits back into the business even to maintain its size as it currently exists. Sometimes, there can be a big difference between a company's reported accounting profitability and its free cash flow. Free cash flow is the amount of cash that a company has left at the end of the year after paying the costs of its operations and making the capital investments necessary to maintain and renew its business. Free cash can then be used by the company to, for example, invest in its growth (organically or through acquisitions), reduce debt, or return cash to shareholders through dividends or share buybacks. The sum of all the free cash generated by the company in the future, discounted back to its present value, then gives us an idea as to the intrinsic value of the company.

When we developed our valuation model for CVE, oil prices naturally and quite expectedly played the biggest role. It is easy to change at will the price input to the model, however, and we were able to calculate the intrinsic value of CVE for different variations of the oil price. We also were able to calculate what oil price is implicitly reflected in the CVE share price today. For a long-term oil price (WTI) of $60, we estimate that CVE will generate free cash flow of CAD 18 billion over the five years, 2024–2028. An oil price of $60 would be below our estimated incentive price level, however, and we regard it as unsustainable in the long term. If we substitute an oil price of $75 into the model, then we find that CVE should generate free cash flow of CAD 30 billion over the five years. That's 60% of the company's current market capitalization, and the average free cash flow yield (the ratio of free cash flow to market capitalization) over that time would be 12%. That's an attractive yield, and yet we still think of the $75 oil price as being below the long-term incentive price. Applying our valuation model in reverse, we find that CVE's current share price, which values the entire company at CAD 42 billion, implicitly assumes a long-term oil price of around $50 per barrel, which we believe is too low. Such a long-term oil price would imply too little investment in the development of new production capacity, and the balance between supply and demand could be achieved only if there was a significant long-term drop in demand. As I have written in this chapter and in the previous chapter, we regard this as highly unlikely. We consider continuing growth in oil demand to be a much more likely scenario. This growth will require a much higher price to balance oil consumption and production. In such an environment, CVE should do well.

It is important still to comment upon CVE's preferred asset allocation. Whenever we find a company that is generating a large surplus of free cash, it is extremely important to keep a sharp eye on how management handles that cash. If handled poorly and inefficiently, then value will be destroyed, and the value previously created by the company's own business activities may be largely lost. If, however, management handles free cash efficiently and rationally, it can deliver even greater additional value to shareholders in this way. What priorities has CVE management set for the allocation of free cash? In the spring of 2021, CVE completed the acquisition of its Canadian competitor Husky Energy. Thereafter, CVE management announced the following asset allocation guidelines: If CVE's net debt is above CAD 8 billion, free cash will be used to reduce debt. If net debt is between CAD 4 billion and CAD 8 billion, half of the free cash will go to debt reduction, and half will be paid out to shareholders. Once net debt reaches CAD 4 billion, 100% of the free cash will go to shareholders. CVE management has adhered to this plan for the past three years. In July 2024, net debt dropped to CAD 4 billion for the first time, and since then, all free cash has been going to shareholders. CVE pays a rather small dividend and prefers to buy back shares at the current share price. In the past two years before reaching the CAD 4 billion net debt threshold, CVE repurchased approximately 8% of its own shares. This rate is expected to have at least doubled from August 2024. Adding in the dividend brings us to a double-digit percentage of the market capitalization and thus roughly our expected free cash flow yield as estimated for a $75 oil price. If management sticks with this asset allocation strategy through the next few years, it should deliver significant per-share value growth for shareholders.

Investments in the petroleum sector stand outside the interest of passive investors, mainly due to the companies' small weightings in the major indices. They are also relatively unpopular with many investors, for whatever reasons. Analyses of these companies are laborious, data-intensive, and work for experienced analysts. They require investors to have a fair level of confidence in their own judgment, as the market consensus is often quite at variance, and the high volatility of oil prices and production company share prices make it difficult to distinguish between information and noise. Precisely for these reasons, however, interesting investment opportunities may exist. Such opportunities not only can provide attractive returns but also can play an important diversification role within an investment portfolio, including as a hedge against certain types of extreme risk. It is up to each individual investor to decide whether they are willing to go to the work and effort required to find these opportunities. One of the investment theories that deals with capital cycle analysis states that the profitability of a sector and the amount of capital investment in that sector are negatively correlated. Investors should therefore prefer companies in sectors from which capital is being withdrawn to those that are drowning in a flood of capital inflows. Indeed, capital flows significantly affect the balance between supply and demand and, consequently, firms' profitability and returns on capital. The oil and gas exploration and production sector is precisely such a place where these considerations can be applied when choosing investments.

Chapter 12

KLA Corporation

Seeking Treasure Among Technology Companies

We now move on from a relic of the past – dirty oil – to the sterile technology environment of the future and the world of zeros and ones. Is it possible to find value among technology companies, a popular sector? An old investment maxim says that only unpopular assets can be truly cheap. Indeed, unpopularity, investor disinterest, and underappreciation for certain companies or sectors do go hand in hand with low share prices. Technology stocks scarcely can be seen as unpopular, uninteresting, or underappreciated among investors. On the contrary, we see the exact opposite. These companies are at the center of attention, many investors can hardly talk about anything else, and such high expectations are attached to some companies that it would be difficult ever to fulfill them.

What Exactly Is a Technology Company?

Companies traded on the stock markets are divided into 11 different sectors. MSCI and S&P Dow Jones Indices developed the Global Industry Classification Standard (GICS) for companies in 1999 to provide a consistent set of definitions for stock sectors and their underlying industry groups, industries, and subindustries. Within this classification, each company is assigned a single GICS classification according to its core business. Two of the 11 sectors include companies that can be classified as technology companies. The first is the sector called Information Technology, abbreviated as IT. The IT sector contains some of the largest companies in the S&P 500, including the likes of Microsoft, Apple, Nvidia, Broadcom, Oracle, and Salesforce. Companies in this sector produce software applications and provide services and infrastructure such as data centers, cloud computing, and so forth. They also manufacture hardware and devices like personal computers, mobile telephones, servers, and routers. Finally, the sector includes manufacturers of semiconductors and related products.

The second sector embracing technology companies is Communications Services. This is a fairly new sector that was introduced in September 2018 as a reclassification of the sector previously called telecommunications. Up to that time, the telecommunications sector had been shrinking down to a few companies providing traditional fixed and wireless communications services, such as Verizon and AT&T, after years of consolidation. The change in 2018 brought media companies that both distribute and produce content, such as Netflix and Walt Disney, into the sector, as well as companies involved in advertising, print and digital publishing (newspapers, magazines, books), and interactive home entertainment (including mobile gaming apps). It has also added interactive media and services, including large search engine and social media companies like Alphabet (parent company of Google) and Meta (parent company of Facebook) – companies that are today regarded as being among the leaders in artificial intelligence (AI) research. (For the record, Amazon is in the Consumer Discretionary sector.) Together, the two sectors occupy about 40% of the S&P 500's market capitalization and comprise 86 companies. From a global perspective, the entire segment of technology companies is America-centric. Of the world's 50 largest among these companies by market capitalization, as many as 80% are U.S.-based. The United States is clearly dominant in this respect.

I would not look for the answer to the question of what a technology company is just in its affiliation with the two sectors mentioned. On one hand, this group is too broad and heterogeneous; on the other, it is at the same time too restrictive. The Wikipedia definition of a technology company is also unclear and restrictive. It says this: "A technology company is an electronics-based technology company, including, for example, businesses relating to digital electronics, software, and Internet-related services, such as e-commerce services." In my opinion, this definition is too narrow and actually excludes a number of companies that have developed and use various modern, advanced, and boundary-pushing technologies.

A narrow view of the definition as to what is a technology company will be confirmed by even a casual Internet search. When I asked which technologies are considered "top trending" today, I got the following list: AI, machine learning, data science, full stack development, robotic process automation, edge computing, virtual reality, blockchain, 5G, and cybersecurity. All are essentially about software and working with data, and the list completely leaves out activities where something is actually being produced, as if the technologies that exist or are being developed to do such things are inferior.

Many companies today try to present themselves as technology companies because they believe that this will cause them to be seen in a better light and make them more attractive to investors. This naming game is similar to a mania we saw 25 years ago, when all one had to do sometimes was to append a ".com" to a company name and the stock price would go up. Today, the suffix "tech" is being added to various activities. This has given rise to a number of seemingly new industries: BigTech, FinTech, RegTech, GovTech, GastroTech, FoodTech, InsuranceTech, HealthTech, TransportTech, AgroTech. Unfortunately, this often is mostly a case of form over substance. Some companies' persistent efforts to present themselves as "tech" even when it's pretty dubious as to whether they are really doing anything new raises legitimate questions as to just how useful the term is.

Meanwhile, there are a great many advanced and critically important technologies in such nontech segments as aerospace and defense, automobiles, photolithography, robotics, oil drilling, 3D printing, nanotechnology, pharmaceuticals, laboratory testing, food processing, and so on. Hardly anyone, however, thinks of the representatives of these industries and the companies involved in the development and use of these technologies, be they Lockheed Martin, Airbus, Boeing, Toyota, BMW, Bosch, Fanuc, Roche, LabCorp, Nestle, Codelco, or Halliburton, as technology companies. Yet, these companies are largely built on advanced and modern technologies. What, for example, is the difference between ASML and Lockheed Martin? ASML is a Dutch company with products at the cutting edge of technological advancement. The company's flagship products are machines that produce chips by printing them in layers on top of one another using light. This process is called *lithography*. A lithography system is essentially a projection system. Light is projected through a plan of the pattern to be printed (known as a *mask* or *mesh*). The plan is four times larger than the intended pattern on the chip. When the pattern is encoded in light, the system's optics shrink it and focus it onto a light-sensitive silicon wafer. Once the pattern has been printed, the system shifts the wafer slightly and produces another copy on it. This process is repeated until the wafer is covered with patterns, completing one layer of chips on the wafer. To produce an entire microchip, this process is repeated 100 times or more, and the patterns are superimposed. The size of the printed elements varies depending on the layer, which means that different types of lithography systems are used for different layers, from the latest-generation extreme ultraviolet light (EUV) systems for the smallest elements to older deep ultraviolet light (DUV) systems for the largest ones. The most advanced range of EUV machines can work with 2 nm chip sizes. ASML is classified in the technology sector, and, as it is directly involved in semiconductor manufacturing, this will surprise no one, but it is worth noting that ASML's core technology lies in the manufacturing process, and the result is a tangible product.

Not many investors think of Lockheed Martin as a technology company. Within the Industrials sector, it is further classified as Aerospace & Defense. Yet, many of its products use sophisticated and advanced technologies. Lockheed Martin's flagship product is the fighter jet. The most advanced of these, the F-35 fighter, the price of which is about the same as that of some of ASML's EUV machines, can easily rank among the most technologically advanced products on the planet. When one delves into learning about it and wondering about the various technologies used in its production and operation, terms like *VLO Stealth, Weapons Capacity, Supersonic Speed and Extended Range, Sensor Fusion, Network Enabled Ops, Electronic Warfare System, Sensor Suite*, and the like start to jump out at you. The plane embodies a complex combination of technologies that relate to the manufacturing process, materials and their properties, radio communications, electronics, software, computing, and so on. If ASML is considered a technology company primarily because it uses complex and advanced technologies in the manufacture of its machines, then the same can be said of Lockheed Martin and many other companies.

This is how we as investors try to view technology companies – not by what sector they are formally classified within but by whether the technologies and processes used in the production of their products and services constitute a significant element in value creation or a source of sustainable competitive advantage. Among the companies that are formally classified as technology companies and fall into either the Information Technology or the Communications Services sector, there are some that can be said to be just that but also some for which such designation is at least questionable. Likewise, among the companies that do not formally belong to these two sectors, there are many that are clearly built to a large extent on technology and that base their market positions and competitiveness upon it.

Reasons for Caution

Technology companies are often the focus of investor interest. This is nothing new. This inclination can be traced back to the years before World War I. Technology companies often symbolize progress, a way forward, or optimism, and for investors they can also mean excitement, adrenaline, or a feeling of contributing to the development of something new. In many cases, such investments later turn out to have been well chosen. History is also full of cautionary tales, however, about investing in new technology waves, and it may be good to learn from them. I will summarize the cautionary historical experiences in three main points.

First, the popularity of an asset often goes hand in hand with a high market valuation for the stock. True bargains are usually found in assets that are neglected or underappreciated. This is usually not the case with technology companies. It is good to remember that share price always matters. Company XYZ, for example, which is the clear and widely recognized leader in a new technology field, can be a great investment at price A, a mediocre investment at price 2 × A, and a lousy investment at price 3 × A. A good company is not the same as a good investment. This is an old truth that is most often forgotten.

Second, investors often tend to overestimate the importance of innovation in the period in which they are investing. We commonly hear that the past two decades have brought an unprecedented amount of major innovation and that the pace of development and progress is gathering speed. We heard the same at the turn of the century with the advent of the Internet, and now we are hearing it with the dawning of artificial intelligence. But is the current pace of innovation really record-breaking? My fellow Czech Václav Smil, who is one of the world's leading generalist scientists (a rare and endangered species, by the way), argues that today's pace of innovation cannot, for example, even remotely compare to the innovations that came into the world in the 1880s. In a few short years, inventions such as the first Edison power station in London, the first hydroelectric power station, the steam turbine, the four-stroke internal combustion engine, the first steel-framed skyscraper, and the first electromagnetic waves created in a laboratory all saw the light of day. The impact of these innovations on developments in society, and in such rapid succession, will be difficult to match today. Smil also points out that, in fact, today's modern innovations are only variants of two earlier fundamental discoveries: microprocessors (developed by Texas Instruments in 1958) and the use of radio waves (first used by Heinrich Hertz in 1885).

I clearly remember the groundbreaking importance assigned to the boom of the Internet more than 25 years ago. It was expected to be a significant driver of labor productivity. However, when I look at the curves that show labor productivity growth in the most developed countries, what surprises me is not that the rates of that growth are declining in the long run, which they are, but that we do not find the expected upswing in labor productivity growth rates in the period around the advent of the Internet and during its subsequent rapid development. The significance of the current innovations can be assessed only with the benefit of hindsight, and it is hard to say in advance whether the initial hopes will be realized.

Third, investors often get excited about the next generation of technology companies, pointing out how quickly they are replacing the generation of companies that until recently have been kings of the hill. Often forgotten is the historical experience, which urges caution. When we look back at what is happening in the markets, not just decades ago but perhaps even a century in the past, we see a recurring phenomenon. Whenever a new wave of technological innovation came along, it is true that it brought along a new generation of technology companies that pushed out of the market most of the representatives of the previous "ruling" generation and took their place. For some time, it seemed that these companies would be the future and that nothing would threaten their strong, often dominant positions. However, this was true only until the next new wave of technological change, the next new generation of companies, and the significant retreat of the incumbents from their positions. If part of the appeal of technology companies is that they represent progress, change, and something new, then that, too, is part of their risk. Change, progress, and the emergence of new technologies will continue, and new waves of change will likely bring new technology leaders. Of the older ones, some may adapt and survive successfully, but many will gradually descend from the first league to the second, third, and perhaps much lower, as has been the case almost since time immemorial. Technology companies represent an interesting area for active investing, and analysis of technology companies is well worth the time and effort. It is also a sector that hides many risks, however, and a common outcome of analyzing a technology company can be that the investor is unable to predict with sufficient certainty the probabilities as to how the company may develop in the longer term and what will be its future free cash flow trajectory. Investors' ability to estimate with high probability that a sufficiently wide margin of safety lies between a technology stock's price and its value, that necessary step preceding any fundamentally based investment thesis, is often weak. A great many technology companies may therefore end up in what Charlie Munger called the "too hard pile."

Charlie Munger used to describe Berkshire Hathaway as having three piles of companies: yes, no, and too hard. He described how, when looking for potential investments for Berkshire's portfolio, he and Warren Buffett proceeded by gradually narrowing down the existing set of companies through three basic filters. First, they'd eliminate those companies not falling within their "circle of competence" and where they didn't feel they had an advantage as investors. Next, they'd try to avoid securities that they believed showed signs of potential catastrophic risk, companies that exhibited high levels of either balance sheet risk, business risk, or valuation risk. Finally, they avoided securities that fell into the "too hard" pile, such as companies that are difficult to analyze and understand, that are struggling with structural and business issues, or that have management teams with which Berkshire could not identify. Munger added that their "too hard" pile may be someone else's "easy pile" and vice versa. They often found the best ideas when they looked at unfollowed and unpopular parts of the market. In other words, in other people's "too hard" piles. When analyzing technology companies, most investors are digging into the too hard pile and shouldn't be afraid to admit that. This admission is a key element to managing risk in investing.

Invisible Oligopolies

Through Vltava Fund's more than 20 years in existence, a number of technology companies have appeared in our portfolio. We still hold several today, and one of them is KLA Corporation (KLAC). Although much of semiconductor manufacturing has moved outside the United States over the past few decades, there are several companies in America without which (or perhaps without Tokyo Electron of Japan and the Dutch ASML) it would be almost impossible to manufacture advanced types of semiconductors in the world. These include a group of three companies, each with a dominant global position in its field, which operate more or less as oligopolies. They are Lam Research, Applied Materials, and KLA Corporation. Lam Research specializes in "etching." In semiconductor manufacturing, etching refers to any technology that selectively removes material from a thin layer on a substrate (with or without pre-existing structures on its surface) and, through this removal, creates a pattern of that material on the substrate. Applied Materials develops, manufactures, and sells a range of manufacturing equipment used to produce semiconductor chips. KLA Corporation has a dominant global position and the best tools and techniques to detect nanometer-sized (i.e., really small) defects in fabricated semiconductors and lithography masks.

The semiconductor manufacturing cycle can be broken down into three phases: design, actual manufacturing, and testing. Production of the most advanced semiconductors requires several hundred individual steps, some of which require many repetitions. Most chips consist of two main structures: a lower structure, usually composed of transistors or capacitors, which performs the "smart" functions, and an upper "interconnect" structure, usually made up of circuits, which connects the components in the lower structure. After each layer is fabricated, each chip on the wafer is tested for functionality. The wafer is then cut into individual chips, and the chips that pass the functionality testing are packaged. Final testing is performed on all the packaged chips. KLA Corporation focuses on the control of the manufacturing process and inspection of the manufactured semiconductors at various stages of the manufacturing process. This is a highly technologically demanding and specialized activity. KLAC has a global market share of 57% and is four times the size of its nearest competitor, according to data from consultancy Gartner. KLAC's main customers are such major semiconductor manufacturers as Taiwan Semiconductors and Samsung Electronics. KLAC's business depends on the capital expenditures of semiconductor companies and the demand for products that use semiconductors. It is cyclical, although somewhat less so than is semiconductor manufacturing itself. Nevertheless, cyclicality must be taken into account, and any imbalance between supply and demand in the semiconductor market can sometimes produce dramatic fluctuations. Moreover, risk is inherent in the type of business that KLAC does. The market for yield management and process monitoring is characterized by rapid technological development and product innovation. Failure to develop new products and technologies in a timely manner in response to changing market conditions could impact KLAC's business. Paradoxically, this is also where lies a part of KLAC's competitive advantage. KLAC's competitors are exposed to the same risk, but because they have much smaller market shares, they are also less well placed and have fewer resources and incentives to invest into development. The longer I follow KLAC (but also, for example, ASML, Applied Materials, Taiwan Semiconductors, or Lam Research), the more I get the impression that know-how and technological maturity are highly cumulative by nature. This is much more the case than in other industries, and it can be an important source of competitive advantage. Indeed, for leaders in their fields, this advantage can have a growing tendency.

In the long term, however, market developments should continue to provide strong wind to KLAC's sails. Semiconductor capital spending is in the middle of a technology cycle that is influenced by 3 nm/2 nm Foundry/Logic technology, sub-15 nm DRAM, and high layer count 3D NAND. As the complexity of device manufacturing increases, the need to analyze defects and metrology issues at critical points in integrated circuit manufacturing processes increases significantly. In addition, as advanced chip designs become more sensitive to subtle changes in manufacturing, it is essential to monitor critical areas within the chip design framework. The combination of end-market expansion, increased market share, and technological leadership, as well as high margins and returns on capital, should combine to deliver above-average earnings growth for KLAC over the long term. KLAC is a company that is much less talked about than are the major players in either semiconductors or technology generally, but it stands at a critical point in the manufacturing process for products that are riding and likely will continue to ride a secular growth wave for a long time. It is another hidden investment treasure.

I think KLAC has a strong long-term sustainable competitive advantage. This is mainly attributable to market share combined with the technological level of its proprietary services. The existence of a competitive advantage is also evidenced by a look at the company's financial statements. The return on capital is close to 40%, the gross margin at 60%, and the net margin above 30%. The capital intensity of KLAC's business is relatively low. Capex of approximately $300 million is a low number for a company with sales of $10 billion and net income of more than $3 billion. Free cash flow is close to net profit. A certain downside, although most other companies would be grateful for it, is that KLAC doesn't have many opportunities to invest the free cash. In 2018, KLAC bought Orbotech for $3.4 billion. This diversified KLAC's end market a bit, but otherwise KLAC makes acquisitions rather smaller in size and relatively infrequently. I consider that a plus. It can grow organically with the industry, but because its market share is already large, KLAC's prospective further growth is likely to be gradual. KLAC therefore returns its spare cash to shareholders. In addition to a small dividend, this is mainly through buying back shares. Over the past five years, the number of shares outstanding has fallen by 15% thanks to share buybacks. That's nice, but the prices at which buybacks occur are sometimes so high that one must question whether they are adding value for existing shareholders or destroying it. In our portfolio, KLAC is one of the smaller positions and one of the most expensive as measured by the likes of P/E or free cash flow yield (FCFY). Indeed, even regarding the best companies, we are constantly reminded that the price at which one buys them matters a lot. Share price can make one and the same company either a great investment or a completely lousy one.

Chapter 13

JPMorgan Chase and OSB Group

Seeking Treasure Among Banks

Many investors avoid investing in bank stocks. They have various reasons, ranging from the more sophisticated ones, such as due to the regulation of the sector, its use of leverage, and strong competition or systemic risk, to more simplistic ones, such as the belief that banks in general will soon disappear and that they are just black boxes with no possibility to know what is inside. Some reasons are rational, but often convenience, lack of knowledge, and prejudices play a role. On the other hand, there are many successful investors who have been investing in bank shares with good results throughout their careers. One of them is Warren Buffett. As with any other investment, things are not black and white with banks, but truth lies somewhere in the middle. In my opinion and in our practical experience, the banking sector offers active investors a broad field for exploration. The fact that a large number of investors avoid banks offers a good start. A well-chosen bank stock can bring investors an attractive return, even a return that is well above the market average. But this doesn't come for free. It takes quite a bit of work. If you've already read this far in the book, this won't surprise you, however, and I believe it's something even to look forward to. So, how does one get started?

Valuation of Banks

First, it's a good idea to understand what banks do, how they make their money, which ratios and other indicators derived from their financial statements are especially useful to look at, and how to interpret them. Then, it is important to understand that the approaches used to value bank stocks cannot be the same as those used to value nonfinancial companies. Once an investor is fitted out with this theoretical foundation, then the next step is to analyze, say, 50–60 banks from all around the world and banks of different types – large U.S. banks, European banks, Japanese banks, midsize and regional banks, banks from various emerging markets, broadly focused banks, and narrowly specialized banks, investment banks, and so on. That will give the investor a good overview of the industry to see that there are big differences between banks, countries, and types of banks, to get an idea of how the industry works, including its dynamics and potential. Last but not least, they will acquire an overview of the valuations at which bank shares trade. One will observe the differences between countries, between different types of banks, and the differences in various situations across the economic and market cycle. On the face of it, this may seem like a lot of work to some, and it is certainly not done in just a matter of a few months. The result, however, can be a surprising discovery that the banking sector is not nearly so complex for investment as it might initially appear and that it is possible to navigate it well with relatively little effort. The knowledge that an investor builds from studying the banking sector in the first few years can benefit them for decades to come.

It is not possible to use valuation models that build on free cash flow in order to value banks as they are used for nonfinancial companies. This is because free cash flow is difficult to estimate for banks. It is problematic in the case of banks to determine such items as capital spending, working capital, and debt. A look at the financial statements of a typical bank will show that almost all items on the balance sheet are financial in nature. We don't find production lines, large tangible assets, inventories, logistics centers, high research and development outlays, and the like. When banks do invest, these investments are largely in people or into their brands. Most of these investments are from an accounting point of view reflected in the current year's costs. In the cash flow statements, capital spending is small. Moreover, it is quite difficult to estimate what part of that is of a growth nature and what part is merely investment into asset renewal. Estimation of free cash flows is further complicated by the frequent large movements in current assets and liabilities and by the fact that it is difficult to define the amount of debt for banks. This is not difficult for nonbanks. The difference between equity and debt is in their cases obvious. With banks, it's more complicated. Moreover, in the case of banks, debt is fundamental to their existence and functioning. Deposits are usually the largest liability (debt) of banks, but without deposits a normal bank cannot function. Not all deposits are equal in terms of how they are defined as debt either. Other items commonly encountered on the liability side for a bank are liabilities to other banks, including the central bank, short-term debt, long-term debt, and trade payables. Then there is a gray area at the liability/ equity margin, which may contain various preference shares or hybrid capital. Determining with precision for a bank just what is and is not actually debt can be almost impossible. Banks have several layers of liabilities in various forms, and they can exceed by many times the bank's own equity, but they are a standard part of the bank's functioning. The interest costs on all types of debt are enormous for a bank, forming one of the largest items on the expense side, but these must be viewed quite differently from the interest costs of nonfinancial corporations.

Hence, it is not possible to determine the bank's free cash flow or the amount of its investments into growth, or unambiguously to define the amount of its debt. Therefore, a different valuation model must be used. Instead of a model based on free cash flow estimates, we use a valuation model for banks that is based on the balance sheet, the amount of its equity, and the return on that equity. We will try to turn the initial problem we encountered (i.e., the impossibility of estimating free cash flow) to our advantage. If the bank does not have large tangible assets and large capital expenditures, then this means that the amount of annual earnings translates almost exactly into an increase in equity. There is no outflow of cash for large investment needs. In addition, because a large proportion of the items on the bank's balance sheet are valued according to market prices, the return on equity (ROE) is more telling here than is the return on equity for nonfinancial corporations, for which ROE is measured against the historical cost of the assets as corrected for depreciation. The key to valuing a bank is not its earnings, dividend, or earnings growth. Rather, it is the return on equity that we believe the bank will achieve on average over the long term. In the long run, the return earned on shares will be close to the long-term return on the bank's equity. I will outline some simple examples in the following paragraphs.

If a bank has a long-term return on equity (ROE) of 10%, pays no dividends, and reinvests all profits each year, then after 10 years its equity will be 2.59 times what it was at the beginning. This corresponds exactly to a growth rate of 10% per year. If the shares trade at the same multiple of book value (P/BV) at the beginning and at the end of the period, then the return they provide also will be 10% per annum. At a long-term ROE of 6%, after 10 years, equity will be 1.79 times what it was at the start. At an ROE of 17%, it will be 4.8 times what it was at the start, and so on. (Note: return on tangible equity [ROTE] and price to tangible equity [P/TB] multiple can be used in place of ROE and P/BV. The results from the two approaches are usually similar.)

If a bank pays out a portion of its earnings in dividends each year and reinvests the rest, then its equity will grow at a rate equal to ROE reduced by the dividend payout ratio. With an ROE of 10% and a dividend payout equal to half of earnings each year, equity will grow only at a rate of 5% per year. In addition, of course, the investor receives a dividend each year, and that can be reinvested in the purchase of additional shares in the bank. If this situation repeats itself year after year, then the number of bank shares held by the investor will rise and the dividends received will also rise. How much the investor's return differs from the bank's long-term ROE will then depend upon the amount that the investor must pay in taxes on dividends (a big handicap) and the price at which they are able to reinvest the dividends.

When a bank buys back its own shares and some of the profits go to shareholders in this manner, as in the case of dividend payments, this will slow the growth of equity. As investors, however, we are interested not in the total equity of the bank but in the equity per issued share and even more in the intrinsic value of the company per share. In both cases, it will depend upon the prices at which the bank buys back its shares. If it buys them back at below book value, this increases the book value of the remaining shares. Purchases of shares at prices above book value reduce the book value of the remaining shares. Buybacks have a similar effect on the intrinsic value of shares, depending upon whether they are repurchased at prices above or below that intrinsic value. If the intrinsic value of the shares lies above book value, which is the case for banks that have high ROEs, then share repurchases at above book value can simultaneously decrease the book value of the shares but increase the intrinsic value of the shares. A slightly more complex situation arises when a bank simultaneously buys back its own shares and pays dividends. However, common sense or a few numbers scribbled on a napkin are usually sufficient to estimate the impact from this combination of returning capital to shareholders.

Essentially, these are always communicating vessels. If a bank wants to grow quickly, it usually has to reinvest most of its profits into its further development and does not have a large surplus of capital to return to shareholders. Banks have to comply with a whole set of capital adequacy rules, and rapid growth logically implies greater capital requirements. If a bank is growing slowly, either by choice or because of market events, then it often generates surplus capital that it does not need and can return to shareholders through dividends and share buybacks. The growth of its own equity may be much slower, but its growth in equity per share, inclusive of reinvested dividends, may still be greater than that of a rapidly growing bank.

To obtain a long-term return close to the bank's long-term ROE, an investor must not overpay when buying shares. Sure, it's nice if a bank's high ROE causes a bank's book value per share to triple over the course of a decade, but if an investor buys shares at four times the book value at the beginning and 10 years later they are trading at twice the book value, then the movement in the market pricing of the share will completely negate the growth in equity and the impact of the high ROE. As always in investing, price matters. So, how do you estimate a reasonable price for a bank's stock?

This is of course a subjective matter, and different investors may have completely different ideas about it. I'll explain how we approach this at Vltava Fund. Our standard discount rate for stock valuation is 10% per annum. This is our minimum acceptable return when looking for individual equity investments. So, if we expect a bank to have a long-term ROE of 10%, then we see its intrinsic value at 1× book value. We would therefore consider buying shares at prices below book value (i.e., P/BV < 1) so that we have a sufficient margin of safety. If the bank has an ROE above 10%, then our idea of the intrinsic value of its shares is likely also to be above book value (i.e., P/BV > 1). We avoid bank stocks with

ROEs below 10%. While it is true that a bank with a lower ROE could be an attractive investment if we were able to buy its shares at well below their book value, for such an investment to yield an attractive return a valuation correction would need to occur relatively quickly. The longer that correction took, the more the low ROE and slow growth in value would play a role in the overall return. For banks with high ROEs, time is on the investor's side; for banks with low ROEs, it is the other way around. We see a rather close relationship between a bank's ROE and the intrinsic value of its shares relative to their book value. The empirical data from the markets are consistent with this. The correlation between the P/BVs of bank stocks and their ROEs is clear and is evident both across markets and over time. The challenge for the investor is to find attractive anomalies within this data. These appear quite often because the markets are not adequately efficient for this not to be the case. There are other things to consider besides purely financial data. For example, regulatory changes sometimes enter significantly into the valuation of a bank. Most often these are changes relating to capital adequacy, but central bank monetary policy or restrictions on capital distribution also can play a role. Different banks also have different business risk, different levels of financial leverage, different credit risk, different levels of liquidity, different capacity to absorb loss, and perhaps even different sensitivity to the business cycle itself. Generally speaking, a riskier bank should trade at a lower valuation multiple (P/BV) than does a less risky bank. We can reflect all of this into our ideas as to a reasonable multiple of price over book value. Still, it is good not to overcomplicate things. The investor's job is not to build an elaborate model in Excel while trying to prove that the stock is undervalued by 5%. We know from experience that the more sophisticated the valuation model, the poorer the investment outcome. It is much better to wait for situations where a stock's cheapness is so blatant that no further complex calculations are needed. Such times will come around, but one needs to be prepared for them based upon knowledge of the banking sector and individual banks.

The Giant and the Dwarf

We currently have two banks in the Vltava Fund portfolio, JPMorgan and OSB Group. Why did we choose these two out of the hundreds of banks on the market? Each represents an opposite end of the spectrum of bank stocks. Based on our own experience gained through more than 20 years of actively studying banks and investing in their shares, we have come to hold the opinion that if there is to be a bank in our portfolio, then it is a good idea to focus only upon the best of those available. The banking sector is not exactly a place where it pays to compromise on quality just because the stocks of lower quality and therefore of riskier banks are (or only appear to be) cheaper. In the banking sector, long years of relatively great prosperity are often interspersed with short and dramatic periods when banks as a whole perform poorly and even suffer large losses. Similar developments can be expected in the future, and it is therefore necessary to acquire the shares of a bank that has an exceptionally strong resilience in these situations.

The strongest and most resilient global bank is JPMorgan (JPM). It is by far the best managed of the big banks. This is largely down to Jamie Dimon, who has been at the helm for more than 20 years. Dimon is the greatest living legend among bankers, and his track record is outstanding. In March 2000, he took the helm of Bank One. It merged with JPMorgan Chase four years later, and Dimon still runs it to this day. The stock's return (including dividends) since his appointment as CEO at Bank One is a whopping 12.1% per year (1,400% overall) as of the end of 2023. The S&P 500 index has returned 6.9% per year (389% overall) over the same period and the S&P Financials index, which is made up of financial services companies, just 4.9% per year (209% overall). JPMorgan's stock returns measured only since the merger with Bank One in 2004 also have outperformed those of the S&P 500 index. A good bank stock can significantly outperform stock indices because the capital accumulation driven by a bank's high ROE runs much faster than the rate at which stock markets grow over the long term. This does require two fundamental conditions: that the ROE is really high and that the run of compound interest is not disrupted by losses in periods of crisis. JPMorgan satisfies both conditions. JPM's management considers return on tangible equity (ROTE) to be the key indicator of the bank's profitability. It differs from ROE in that it excludes certain types of assets from equity, primarily so-called goodwill. ROTE is therefore slightly higher than ROE, but it can be treated in the same way as is ROE for valuation purposes. The valuation of a bank measured by the ROTE multiple will be slightly higher, but because ROTE is slightly higher than ROE and tangible equity is slightly smaller than equity more generally, the intrinsic share price will be similar in both cases.

JPMorgan's average ROTE since the merger with Bank One is 15.5% per year. This is the rate at which the bank's capital is accumulating before dividend payments and share buybacks. The lowest ROTE over this period was in 2008, at 6%, the worst year of the Global Financial Crisis. A number of banks did not survive that, and many others made huge losses. JPM was the only major U.S. bank that did not need government assistance, was profitable, and, moreover, helped mitigate the impact of the crisis on the entire financial sector by taking over the failing Bear Stearns in March 2008. Jamie Dimon says he expects JPM to be able to achieve an average ROTE of around 17% measured across the economic cycle. Our own analysis reaches a similar conclusion. Seventeen percent is far greater than what growth can realistically be expected from the stock markets overall, and such a return would mean that JPMs stock will continue significantly to beat the market index. So far, it seems realistic. The average ROTE of the past five years is 19%. When one considers that these five years have included a global pandemic, dramatic inflation, rapidly rising interest rates, falling bond prices, and a U.S. banking crisis, this is a respectable result. Other big banks can only dream of such returns. Banks like Bank of America, Citigroup, and Wells Fargo seem to look upon JPM with due respect. That's not to mention the big European banks (HSBC, BNP Paribas, Banco Santander, Barclays) and the big Japanese banks (Mitsubishi UFJ, Sumitomo Mitsui, Mizuho). In terms of asset size, the four largest Chinese banks are bigger than JPM, but, in terms of quality, creditworthiness, and financial strength, they are no match for JPM. Moreover, we would not consider investing in Chinese banks even in our dreams.

JPM has all the prerequisites to further strengthen its position. I have followed JPM as an investor and as a client for a long time. Yet every three months, when I read the new quarterly results, I am repeatedly amazed at how incredibly strong a bank it is. It is the number-one bank in the United States as measured by deposits (11.3% market share), the number-one corporate and investment bank, the largest credit card issuer by spending and balances, the largest mortgage issuer, the largest auto lender, the largest payments processor, and so on. As time goes on, I feel that its market share and lead over its competitors is getting bigger and more resilient. With equity of $340 billion, a Common Equity Tier 1 (CET 1) capital adequacy ratio of 15.3 and Total Loss-Absorbing Capacity of $534 billion, the numbers are unprecedented in the banking world. JPM's shares were among the first we bought after the big stock market plunge in

March 2020 caused by the COVID pandemic around the world, and so far our expectations have been more than fulfilled.

The second bank we hold in the portfolio is one of our newest positions and may serve as proof, among other things, that there is still no shortage of good investment opportunities in the markets. In fact, I would say that these might even be increasing in number. This investment is in a small British bank, OSB Group. I have said that if one is to consider investing in banks, then it is a good idea to focus only on the best available. That was the case with JPM. I think there is a second way to look for hidden treasures among banks, and that is to zero in on banks having some relatively narrow focus, specializing in a market segment that the big banks are bypassing for some reason, and performing well within that specialization. We consider OSB to be representative of exactly this type of selection. It is a smaller and specialized bank that provides mortgages to professional landlords of predominantly residential buy-to-let properties. It has a long tradition and a strong position in this market segment. Tax changes in the UK since 2016 have made it easier to own a residential property through a nonpublic limited company, and especially if the owner has multiple properties. The traditional big banks have more or less pulled back from lending to professional buy-to-let entrepreneurs, leaving the market opportunity to smaller and specialist institutions such as OSB. We sometimes hear it said that the buy-to-let business is risky, but, in our opinion, this view is not based on reality. We believe buy-to-let is less risky than is lending for owner-occupied properties. OSB's long-term results prove this. Its bad loan reserves are typically in the lower tenths of 1% (approximately 0.25%). This is a low number, and it indicates the low risk of the loans. Moreover, the loans are pledged on properties with an average loan to value ratio of 65%. OSB is a bank whose loans are fully funded by deposits on the liability side and is not dependent on the availability of bond financing or on borrowing in the interbank market. OSB is also remarkably efficient. It has a cost/income ratio of around 30%, which would be the envy of almost any other bank. Long-term ROTE is above 15% and return on equity (ROE) is more or less the same. The bank pays out a large dividend on a regular basis and at the same time buys back its own shares.

During the summer of 2024, OSB's shares could be bought cheaply. Their price below 400 pence (UK shares are quoted in pence) represented a P/E of 4.5× and a dividend yield of 8.5%. The dividends plus share buybacks came to a combined 15% of market capitalization. P/BV was 0.7×. These values show that the stock was trading at a low valuation, especially given the bank's high ROE, low credit risk, and high operating efficiency. It wasn't hard to see that the stock must easily have been worth twice the price. The current price provides a large margin of safety. If the bank actually achieves long-term ROE at levels above 15%, as we expect it will, then the stock's returns should be at least that high, too. Probably, returns will run even higher, as we do not expect the ratio of share price to book value to remain at 70% over the long term. On the other hand, we wouldn't mind if it stayed at that level for a few more years, because large buybacks at prices well below book value would deliver significant value growth to the remaining shareholders.

Another way to look at this investment is that OSB can be bought for much less than what it would cost to build it on a greenfield site or what it would likely be sold for as a whole in a private transaction. Public markets often offer prices that are well below replacement cost and private transaction value, and I regard this as one of their main advantages. You may be asking yourself, how is it possible that OSB's stock is trading so cheaply? We have asked that question as well. In the stock markets, one does not usually find a definitive answer to such questions, but we see the most likely reason as being the fact that such stocks are almost completely ignored by most investors. The investment of passive investors – which means most of the money in the markets – is placed elsewhere. OSB is a smaller bank, a so-called small cap. Passive money mostly avoids these. Such investors mostly shun banking as a sector, too, and, in recent years, they have kept away from UK equities generally. The UK market has been one of the least favored for some years now, and in this respect it has taken over the baton from the Japanese market. Put this all together and it's almost a perfect storm. For us, though, the situation is absolutely ideal, and we can't help but reiterate that we hope the prevalence of passively invested money in the markets will last as long as possible, allowing us to continue to benefit from the existence of cheap stocks and allowing us free rein. Banks are important to the functioning of an economy and of companies and they constitute an important part of the capital markets. Studying and analyzing them can reveal not only interesting investment opportunities for investors but, as a by-product, also can provide a better picture as to the state of the economy and other companies. This knowledge can then be useful in selecting and timing investments in other sectors. Banks take the pulse of the economy.

Chapter 14

Markel Group

Seeking Treasure in a Company That Investors Regard as Boring

In the first chapter of this book, we were focused on Berkshire Hathaway. I described it as a company whose success has long played out right in front of investors and for all to see and yet it is a company not well understood by a large number of those investors. I said that I believe this to be the case for a combination of several reasons. First, Berkshire is quite difficult to understand and analyze. A large portion of investors never get over that hurdle, and in some cases they don't even try. Second, it's a business that doesn't offer much hope to those who want to get rich quick. It provides near certainty of high long-term returns, but who has such patience in the markets today? Moreover, investors generally tend to underestimate the long-term effects of compound interest, and that's exactly what Berkshire Hathaway is all about.

What is equally remarkable is that rather few of Berkshire Hathaway's followers come directly from the business world. Its business model, which delivers extraordinary results, is highly efficient, can be built with little constraint to enormous size, is relatively easy to understand, and theoretically does not prevent anyone from following it. In practice, rather surprisingly, this is not the case. In theory, as the saying goes, there is no difference between theory and practice, but in practice there is. In reality, then, there seems to be a big difference between the art of understanding the Berkshire Hathaway business model and the art of applying it in real life. This requires not only a range of skills and abilities but also enormous patience and long-term vision, because it is something that takes decades to build. This combination is rare in the corporate world.

Just as seemingly every company tried to present itself as a dot-com business in the 1990s, then every second company pretended over the past few years to be a tech business, and today everyone wants to be associated with AI, we find at certain types of companies that management is talking about building another Berkshire Hathaway. Upon closer inspection, however, it almost always becomes clear that this is a business very different and far and away removed from the Berkshire model. Many times, one gets the impression that these management don't know at all what they are talking about. In fact, the sole company among those that are publicly traded that can be said to follow in the footsteps of Berkshire Hathaway, to be successful in doing so, and to have progressed very far along the way is the Markel Group. Although it is far from being of Berkshire quality, this is a business that is so interesting and promising that it makes sense to give it proper attention. Markel has one huge advantage over Berkshire Hathaway. With a market capitalization of $20 billion, its size is far from being a constraint upon its future growth. Our own analytical data for the two companies go back to 2001. Since that time, book value per share, a good indicator of intrinsic value growth for both companies, has grown almost identically by more than 10 times. Specifically, it has grown 10.3 times for Markel and 10.04 times for Berkshire. Over the past five years, however, Markel has lagged a bit behind Berkshire in growing both book value and share price. It is partly for this reason, in fact, that its shares are priced attractively. The last time they were this cheap was during 2009–2013. That's when we first bought in, and Markel has been in Vltava Fund's portfolio ever since. If an investor has a good understanding of Berkshire Hathaway's business model, then analyzing Markel Group will not take too much work. In fact, most things will look familiar and already be known and understood.

Markel will soon celebrate its 100th anniversary. In 1930, Samuel Markel founded the company in the U.S. state of Virginia and began building its insurance business with his four sons. Today, Samuel's grandson, Steven Markel, is chairman of the board. Markel's stock went public with an IPO in 1986 at a price of $8.33 and a total market capitalization of $15 million. From today's perspective, it was a relatively miniscule company. Markel's greatest growth is associated with Tom Gayner, today's CEO. He joined Markel in 1990 as the company's equity portfolio manager. At that time, Markel's market capitalization was still only $40 million, and the stock price was around $20. Today, the stock price is $1,570, and the market capitalization is more than $20 billion.

Markel's Three Engines

In Tom Gayner's words, Markel is a company powered by three "engines." The first of these is insurance and reinsurance. This is the original business upon which Markel began to build its enterprise, gradually expanding through both acquisitions and organic growth to its current form. Today, Markel is the world's leading specialist insurance company. Its insurance operations include the Markel Specialty, Markel International, and Global Reinsurance divisions, as well as the company State National, which provides portfolio protection and program services, and Nephila, which manages investments in insurance-linked securities. Markel is the third-largest U.S. provider of excess and surplus insurance. Annual earned premiums are around $8.5 billion, of which 80% come from the United States and one-eighth from reinsurance. The insurance business itself makes solid profits. Its so-called "combined ratio," a key indicator for insurers defined as the sum of claims incurred and operating expenses measured as a percentage of premiums received, has averaged 95% over the past 10 years. Markel also has a very low loss ratio, which is the percentage of insured claims out of premiums received. Over the long term, it has been right around or just over 60%. The remainder of the combined ratio consists in the so-called "expense ratio," which is a ratio showing what percentage of the premiums received goes to the costs of selling and servicing the policies. This ratio can be regarded as quite high and is a possible place where Markel could focus on improving. In any case, if we consider a 95% combined ratio for Markel's insurers to be a typical level of profitability, then this means that their current ability to generate profits, the company's earning power, from policies alone is $425 million per year. Moreover, it is likely to continue to grow significantly as premiums received also grow. The premiums have more than doubled in the past 10 years. Markel's methodology for creating reserves has been consistently conservative over the long term, with a more or less regular release of excess reserves as the development of claims have generally come in below management's original estimates. In the case of insurance companies, management must always work with estimates as to the levels of claims in association with the policies they offer. Accordingly, they must decide how much and at what prices they are willing to underwrite. Inflation, social inflation, and catastrophes are the main unknowns and the main sources of risk. It is important for management to be realistic and conservative in its estimates and to be willing to slow or even stop growth in the volume of premiums written in situations where there is excess capacity in the market and policy prices are inadequately low. There is nothing worse for an insurance company than to be chasing rapid growth and then, in a few years, being shown to have sold its policies at a loss. Discipline is important in the insurance business. Markel's historical numbers and our own long-term analysis suggest that Markel management has that discipline. Otherwise, we would not have considered investing there at all.

Markel's second engine is investment. Its insurance companies generate float similar to that of Berkshire Hathaway. Markel's investment portfolio, based on the existence of float as a very low-cost source of capital, is now approximately $32 billion. The majority of this portfolio is invested in bonds so that the volume of investments and their duration match the size and length of expected future claims while also generating interest income. Unlike most other insurers, Markel's rather high capital relative to the size of its insurance liabilities allows it also to have a large equity portfolio. Approximately one-third of the investment portfolio is invested in equities. Tom Gayner is a skilled investor, and the long-term returns of Markel's equity portfolio under his hands have exceeded the returns of the S&P 500 index by about 1% point a year for the past 20 years. The remarkable thing is that he is achieving these returns even with a portfolio that is broad and diversified. The largest stock position is Berkshire Hathaway. One would expect nothing less from a company whose CEO often follows the Berkshire model. Next come Alphabet, Amazon,

Brookfield Corporation, Home Depot, Deere & Co, Novo Nordisk, and several dozen other mostly well-known names. I think we can expect the return on the entire combined stock and bond investment portfolio to be close to 5% annually, which, at its current size, would yield nearly $1.5 billion in annual profits.

Markel's third engine is the newest. It's called Markel Ventures, and management began building it in 2005. This consists in a group of private noninsurance businesses and, along with the other two engines, paints a picture of Markel's entire business model following in the footsteps of Berkshire Hathaway. The Markel Ventures portfolio of companies consists primarily of cyclical businesses that operate in various product and industry cycles that can offset one another and reduce returns volatility. Markel management expects these companies to outperform the economy as a whole, as some of them are said to "operate with secular tailwinds at their backs." The Markel Ventures portfolio consists primarily of older-economy companies, with no major exposure to the technology and information sectors. Nine of Markel Ventures' 19 companies are located in Virginia, Markel's home state, with the remaining 10 ventures being situated mostly from the nearby states of North Carolina, South Carolina, Pennsylvania, and Georgia. Markel Ventures has often attracted family-owned businesses, for which ownership within the Markel Group is a good form of continuation because, unlike private equity funds, Markel does not use leverage, tends to hold these investments indefinitely, and provides their managers with essentially full decision-making autonomy.

Together, Markel Ventures have annual sales totaling just over $5 billion a year and can produce an estimated nearly $400 million in annual profits. If we add up the profits of all three parts of Markel and subtract the interest expense on Markel's relatively small debt and its taxes, we arrive at an annual profit of approximately $1.5 billion per year. This level of profits would merit a market capitalization of greater than $20 billion, which is in fact the current market capitalization of the Markel Group. Thirteen times annual earnings is a low valuation for a company that has highly efficient capital allocation, management that truly cares about creating shareholder value, and a business that has been growing at a respectable rate for a long time and is very likely to continue to grow for a long time. Markel regularly publishes long time series of its key metrics in its annual reports. Table 14.1 shows the company's 20-year (2003–2023) average annual growth.

Table 14.1 Selected performance metrics from Markel Group.

Indicator	20-Year CAGR
Total operating income	11%
Gross premiums received	9%
Investment portfolio	9%
Equity	13%
Share price	9%

CAGR = compound annual growth rate.
Source: Markel Group.

These numbers are consistent and at the same time represent a higher growth rate than one would expect from the stock markets, both in terms of share price growth and growth in company profitability overall. Perhaps ironically, given how seemingly boring its business may appear to many investors, Markel is a company that has been growing at an above-average rate over the long term even as its market valuation is significantly below average compared to the broader market. I see Markel's fundamental value on a per-share basis to be above $2,000 today, and I expect the share price to grow over the long term (albeit with larger fluctuations from time to time) at rates as suggested by the percentages in the table. Because of Markel Ventures' growing proportion within Markel as a whole and because these acquisitions are accounted for at acquisition cost, the book value of the Markel Group is becoming progressively less indicative of its fundamental value. Therefore, we prefer to use a sum-of-the-parts valuation, which method values each part of Markel separately and then adds all these parts together.

Baby Berkshire

According to our calculations, Markel Group's profitability has more than doubled over the past decade. Earnings per share have been growing at an even faster rate as shares outstanding have gradually been reduced through buybacks. Markel's management has been increasing these buybacks, particularly over the past three years, as the scissors between share price and intrinsic value have become more and more open. This is exactly what I would imagine that management ideally should do. So, share buybacks, in my eyes, are the fourth engine that works to create value for the company on a per-share basis. Markel's management views share buybacks as a perfectly good and appropriate asset allocation option alongside the others at its disposal. When there is free cash, there are always several options for how to use it. The insurance business takes first priority. There must be sufficient well-invested but liquid assets to serve as a reserve for paying future insurance claims. Markel has a bond portfolio for this purpose. Other asset allocation options (i.e., growth in written premiums, investment into publicly traded equities, debt repayment, investment in Markel Ventures, and share buybacks) lie side by side on the table, and it always depends upon which of these options currently offers the best combination of return and risk. When Markel stock was trading at 1.5–1.7 times book value, share repurchases were small. The closer the share price got to book value in recent years, however, the larger the share buybacks became. Their relative attractiveness increased and management took advantage of this. The ability to allocate capital efficiently is extremely important for long-term investors. It has a huge impact on the value of a company and Markel's management is doing very well in this respect. For us, this was one of the main arguments for investing in Markel shares.

Markel is a typical candidate to be a hidden investment treasure. Because of its medium size, it does not have a large representation in the major indices. In addition, it belongs to the Financial Services sector and the Insurance – Property & Casualty subsector. Passively invested money doesn't flow much into these places. For active investors, moreover, this sector offers the combination of a complex business with many unknown risks, scant hope of making anybody rich quickly, and the fact that it seems, for many, perhaps, incredibly boring. Its appearance at a superficial glance may thus discourage most potential active investors. Upon taking a more careful look inside the company, however, seeing its business model, historical performance, management quality, and overall corporate culture, it becomes easy for one to reach a wholly different conclusion.

When I was in Omaha this May for Berkshire Hathaway's annual meeting, Markel held a brunch the day after at the hotel across the street. These are, of course, two events that are incomparable in size and importance. Around 40,000 people attend Berkshire's annual meeting and completely fill a huge sports arena and adjacent auditorium. Berkshire is a much bigger company than Markel, with far greater fame and prestige and the greatest of investment legends at its head. Nevertheless, as many as

2,000–3,000 people came to the Markel brunch and completely filled the large ballroom and lobby of the Marriott Hotel. It was interesting to see and compare what kind of people came to the two events. Among the 40,000 attendees at the Berkshire meeting were the greats of the American corporate world (Jamie Dimon from JPMorgan, Tim Cook from Apple, Bill Gates from Microsoft), professional investors, amateur investors, the ordinary curious, and quite obviously investors who are now well past retirement age, have made a lot of money from their long-term holdings of Berkshire stock, and came to express their gratitude to their wealth manager. This broad mix of people is reflected in the questions the audience asks of Buffett. Many of them are about everyday life, philosophical in nature, and the questions about the investments themselves tend to be cautious and not very sophisticated.

At the Markel brunch it was very different. There were not many small and amateur investors among the participants, and certainly none of the touristic nature. It was clear that Markel had a very broad base of supporters and that their sophistication was on average at a much higher level than that of Berkshire's followers. The level of questions from the audience and the overall level of debate in the main hall and foyer was much higher at the Markel brunch. While a certain percentage of Berkshire shareholders will be shareholders more or less just because it is Berkshire, this "glamour factor" is not present in Markel's case. For potential investors in Markel stock, this is a plus. Rather than having to pay a premium through the share price for fame and reputation, they can expect a discount associated with lower interest and understanding. "Baby Berkshire" may be one of the more gratifying positions in the portfolios of long-term, patient investors. When I think about Markel as a long-term investment, I realize that what can be gained by buying its stock today will, over time, be just a fraction of the company's total value. Most of the future value will be what management creates by reinvesting the capital earned. If Markel's management continues to perform as well in asset allocation as it has in recent decades, the company's stock could remain a long-term compounder for still a very long time.

Chapter 15

Quálitas Controladora

Seeking Treasure in Emerging Markets

When you read this chapter, you might remark that I really like insurance companies. You won't be far from the truth. In my profession, I have been close to the financial sector almost all my life, and I've observed along the way that some insurance companies can be good long-term value creators. Like banks, insurance companies have no production lines, no large physical assets, no inventories, no logistics centers, no high research and development outlays, and practically no capital investment. Capital accumulation as the main indicator of a company's value can run relatively fast here. I purposefully say "can," because there is a great deal of disparity from one insurance company to another. If one were to look at this just a bit cynically, a person could note that insurance companies mostly offer entirely commodity products. There are minimal differences between individual insurers, and the brand of the insurer plays little role for many of their customers. Yet, there are enormous differences in the business performance of individual insurers. It seems clear that the differences must be in the people who do the work. In that sense, it's similar to the investment fund industry. There are relatively small differences between individual investment funds in terms of their products, although most of them try to differentiate themselves from others. Nevertheless, the investment results of individual funds differ widely. Again, I would attribute this to the human factor.

We find several companies in Vltava Fund's portfolio that are in the insurance business. Berkshire Hathaway and Markel Group are conglomerates with several different parts, but the core business of each is its insurance group. We also hold shares of Elevance Health, which is a health insurance company. The fourth insurance company and essentially the only traditional pure-play insurance business in our portfolio is Quálitas Controladora. Yes, I like insurance companies. Berkshire Hathaway stock was in my personal portfolio almost a decade before we started Vltava Fund in 2004, and so insurance is one of the sectors I have followed and invested in the longest. Moreover, I like insurance products. As a veteran of the financial market, I am well aware that many financial products are more tailored to the preferences of those who offer them than to those of the clients to whom they sell the products, and the general merits and ethics of many financial products can legitimately be called into question. I nevertheless consider the existence of insurance companies and the ability to insure against various risks to be of great benefit to society generally, and I am pleased to be able to participate with our shareholders in their activities. Just try to imagine what life would be like if there were no health insurance, life insurance, property and casualty insurance, or car insurance. People and businesses would face unexpected and often devastating risks and damages with little ability to prevent their consequences.

Investing in Emerging Markets

I did not choose to write about Quálitas Controladora in this chapter because it is an insurance company. I could have easily chosen a company from another industry. I chose it because Quálitas Controladora is the only stock in our portfolio that comes from an emerging market. All the other companies discussed in this book are based in developed markets. In the investing world, a developed market is a country that is one of the most advanced in terms of its economy and capital markets. The country must have high incomes but also openness to foreign ownership, ease of capital movement, and efficient market institutions. These include countries such as the United States, Canada, those in Western Europe, Japan, Australia, and New Zealand. *Emerging markets* is a term that refers to economies that are experiencing significant economic growth and have some, but not all, of the characteristics of a developed economy. Emerging markets are countries that are transitioning from the "developing" to the "developed" phase. The 10 major emerging market economies are (in alphabetical order): Argentina, Brazil, China, India, Indonesia, Mexico, Poland, South Africa, South Korea, and Turkey. Other important emerging markets are Egypt, Iran, Nigeria, Pakistan, Russia, Saudi Arabia, Taiwan, and Thailand.

According to Goldman Sachs, emerging market equities account for about a quarter of the market capitalization of global equity markets. The bank expects this share to grow to 35% by the end of this decade and to approach 50% around 2050. While emerging countries are playing second fiddle by the size of their stock markets, their aggregate economic power is already much greater. According to World Economics, the 24 largest emerging countries account for as much as 50% of global GDP and in recent decades have generated two-thirds of global economic growth. These countries are also home to a majority of the planet's population, and their social and economic development will play a decisive role in determining what global society and the world economy will look like and their future directions.

The typical investor from a developed country has far fewer assets invested in emerging markets than would correspond to their size. Emerging markets are primarily the domains of their own domestic investors, who, in turn, often face restrictions against investing outside of their own countries. Investing in emerging markets carries with it specific risks in addition to the usual investment risks, but, from the perspective of active investors, they are nevertheless productive hunting grounds for hidden investment treasures.

Through the 20 years of our fund's existence, we have devoted a fair amount of time and effort to studying emerging market stock markets and analyzing individual companies. We have made investments in 14 different emerging markets over time. I would briefly summarize our experience by observing that the first and biggest risk is what I call the "foreigner's handicap." Every investor knows best the investment environment within the country in which they live. This gives one a certain, and sometimes quite significant, advantage over foreign investors who would like to invest in what is that person's home market. Sometimes these factors are obvious, but sometimes they are only about subtle nuances, and the foreign investor then has no real idea of his disadvantage.

If a Czech investor intends to invest abroad – and with an almost nonexistent domestic stock market there is no other choice – the Czech investor has the foreigner's handicap. It will be relatively small in markets such as the United States or the United Kingdom. It will be somewhat larger in France or Italy, for example, and greater still in Japan. If he ventures into emerging market investing, the size of his handicap will grow by leaps and bounds. Typical markets where domestic investors have enormous advantages due to their knowledge of the realities on the ground are, for example, India or the countries of South-East Asia.

The second-greatest risk in my eyes is the business and shareholder culture in individual emerging market countries. Every long-term active and value investor is primarily interested in how management creates value for the company on a per-share basis. If management does not see this as its primary objective, then investing in such a company makes little sense. Of course, this problem is not exclusive to emerging markets. Even in developed markets, there are plenty of companies that would not pass through this screen. In some emerging markets, though, it's almost the norm that shareholder value is not a high priority. To put things nicely and make no mention of outright fraud against shareholders, I would just say that we need to avoid investing in companies (and countries) where shareholder value is not a high priority in the eyes of management. Our own investment and analytical experience would include China, for example, among such countries.

A third risk that often causes us to discontinue our contemplations to invest in an emerging market's equities is currency risk. We are not interested in investment returns in the domestic currency of the country in whose market we are placing our money but, rather, in the base currency of our fund. This is the Czech koruna. We hedge most of the currency risk in our investments while taking into account the cost-benefit ratio of doing so. In emerging markets, currency risk is often high. At the same time, hedging that risk can be costly because the interest-rate differential between the two currencies that must be paid to do so is large inasmuch as emerging markets often have high local interest rates. There are then two options: either factor the expected drop in the local currency's value in the expected return of the share or avoid investing in the local currency altogether. Because estimating just how much a local currency might depreciate is necessarily quite imprecise, we therefore exercise the second option in some countries and just avoid investing there. These countries include Turkey, Argentina, and South Africa, for example.

The aforementioned three risks significantly narrow the space that we consider investable in emerging markets. That means our investments here are few and selective. We consider such an investment only if we regard the company involved as quite exceptional in its own way. We view Quálitas Controladora as just such a company. It is Mexico's largest auto insurer. I invested privately in the Mexican market already back in the late 1990s, and we view as acceptable the foreigner's handicap that definitely exists. In terms of shareholder value creation, Quálitas sets an example that many companies in developed markets would do well to emulate. As for currency risk, we are willing to take it in the case of Mexico and, so far, the change in the Mexican peso's value through the period during which we have been holding Quálitas's stock has shown us to be right in doing so. Mexico has benefited strongly in recent years from a trend known as *nearshoring*. During the period when the Coronavirus ravaged the world, numerous supply chains were disrupted, and many companies realized how vulnerable they were. Their natural response is to try to bring both their own production and the individual links in the supply chain closer to their end markets. For large U.S. firms, it is much less risky to produce or to import goods from Mexico, for example, than from China or Vietnam, and, in many cases, it is even less costly. Mexico, its economy, and currency are among the main beneficiaries of this trend. Mexico lies right next to the biggest market. Its manufacturing sector is highly developed and has decades of accumulated experience in manufacturing for the U.S. market. Sales to the U.S. account for 90% of Mexico's exports and exports overall account for 40% of Mexico's GDP. This is twice as much as China, for example. Nearshoring positively affects a wide range of sectors in the Mexican economy – the automotive sector, transport, the steel and chemical industries, the financial sector, and household consumption.

The Mexican stock market is not large. Fewer than 150 companies are traded on the stock exchange. Vltava Fund's only emerging markets investment is currently there. This is not because we want to have any exposure to Mexico per se, but because there's a company here that we like, and the Mexican economic and investment environment does not represent an obstacle. I first learned about Quálitas at the Value Spain investment conference in Madrid. It piqued my interest immediately, so we began to analyze and follow the company, and after two to three years, in 2020, we included it into our portfolio.

Mexican Beauty

Quálitas Controladora is Mexico's largest car insurer. If you were looking for a similar equivalent in the U.S. market, you could look to GEICO, which is owned by Berkshire Hathaway, or the publicly traded The Progressive Corporation. Their long-term earnings track records are phenomenal. But Quálitas may be an even better business, as well as a business with greater potential. In most developed countries, the auto insurance industry is rather mature and slow-growing. Those countries' populations, car numbers, and insurance of cars are growing only slowly. But Mexico is an altogether different story. The population (today about 130 million) may not be growing as fast as it used to be, but it is a relatively younger demographic and, above all, a middle-income country. As a result, it lags behind the high-income countries in the number of cars per capita. Car sales in Mexico are between 1 and 1.5 million annually. In the United States, which has two-and-a-half times the population, around 16 million cars are sold annually. The number of cars sold in Mexico can be expected to rise in the long term.

Another indicator by which the car market in Mexico lags behind developed countries is the insurance of cars. Only about a third of the cars driven in Mexico have insurance. Even though car insurance is compulsory in Mexico, this regulation does not yet seem to be fully respected, and there does not appear to be much enforcement. Improving this situation is likely to be a slow and gradual process. Mexico's car insurance industry has many more growth characteristics than we are accustomed to in developed markets, and we expect that Quálitas will benefit from this for many years to come. Overall, the insurance sector in Mexico represents just 2.5% of

GDP. This is not only much less than in developed countries but also less than in other major Latin American countries such as Colombia, Brazil, and Chile. In fact, it could be said that the entire financial market in Mexico has a much lower penetration of its products than is common in other countries. It is estimated that only half of Mexican adults have bank accounts, 40% have retirement savings, and only one in three Mexicans understands the concept of compound interest (here I would not be so sure that Mexico is an exception).

Quálitas is already the clear industry leader. Its market share is 35% and is about the same as the combined market share of its four largest competitors (GNP, Chubb, AXA, and HDI Seguros). Quálitas has an even greater share of the industry's profitability. In 2023, it accounted for almost 60% of profits for the entire car insurance industry.

Quálitas Controladora's business model is simple and straightforward. The alpha and omega is car insurance in Mexico. The total fleet in Mexico includes about 56 million cars. Quálitas insures approximately 5.5 million of these. That's only one-tenth of all cars, but it is almost one-third of those cars insured. In 2023, the total premiums received by all insurers and auto insurance companies in Mexico totaled 153 billion pesos. Of this, Quálitas accounted for more than 53 billion pesos.

The policies themselves are profitable for Quálitas. Its average combined ratio over the past 10 years is 92%. The industry average is more than 95% (but around 97% if Quálitas is excluded when calculating that average), which means that Quálitas has about a 5% point advantage here. Insuring automobiles differs from other types of insurance in its cost structure. It has a low operating ratio (the ratio of operating costs to premiums received), a low loss ratio (the ratio of claims to premiums received), and high acquisition costs, which are the costs of selling policies. The latter is because most car insurance policies have short duration, usually one year. One of Quálitas's competitive advantages is its distribution network. Most auto insurance policies are sold by independent agents. Quálitas's clear focus on one type of insurance and its excellent reputation in the market for service enables it to build and maintain better relationships with agents than do its competitors.

Another main source of profits for Quálitas, as for most insurance companies, is its investment portfolio. This is quite large, at about 50 billion pesos, and is made up of float from policy sales and other reinvested profits. Almost 90% of this is invested in bonds and the rest in equities.

Information on the exact composition of the equity portfolio is sketchy, but from what I have been able to gather from management, it is a mix of mainly Mexican active and global passive (ETF) investments. In terms of capital strength, Quálitas is in a good position. Quálitas exceeds by almost four times the regulatory minimum that requires insurance companies to hold a certain amount of capital relative to the size of their own businesses. In essence, you could say the company is overcapitalized and doesn't need so much capital. That's true. In the case of insurance companies, however, it is much better to have an excess of capital than to face an insufficiency of capital. Despite its excess capital, Quálitas has a high ROE. Over the past 10 years, ROE has averaged 24%. Management recognizes that it has too much capital and is addressing this by paying a high dividend. It has an internal rule that it will pay out 40–90% of earnings each year in dividends as long as the company's capitalization is at least 1.5 times the regulatory minimum. This condition is amply met and so the dividend can be expected to be more at the upper end of the range. We expect it to be in the range of 60–90% of earnings. As the volume of policies increases, Quálitas's capital requirement also will rise and the high payout ratio will therefore gradually reduce the company's overcapitalization. With its surplus of capital, Quálitas logically has no debt. It doesn't need it.

Quálitas's balance sheet and capital strength are associated with a long-running tax dispute between the Mexican state and the entire insurance industry. It concerns whether insurance companies can take tax credits into account when calculating VAT. The insurance companies do so, and it is a generally established standard practice, but the state wants to dispute it. If the state's position were actually to prevail, the insurance companies would have to pay large amounts of back taxes. In the case of Quálitas, this would reduce its equity and cut into its excess capital. Ironically, however, this might actually improve its market position, because some other insurers might be hit so hard by additional taxes that they would become insolvent.

Quálitas has done share buybacks in the past, but its shareholder structure has hampered the company from doing so. The family of founder Joaquín Brockman Lozano (deceased in 2021) holds 50.1% of the shares and apparently does not want to increase its stake or to reduce the stock's liquidity. A large ownership stake tends to be a barrier to share buybacks in many companies, but often it is offset by its positive impact on the company's operations and management. We generally like companies that are run by the founder, that person's descendants, or a shareholder with a large ownership stake. We have several such companies in the fund's portfolio. In the case of Quálitas, we have a high opinion of management's ability to run the company for the benefit of shareholders and its ability to allocate capital effectively.

A few more details remain to be added to the description of Quálitas's business. Although its main insurance market is Mexico, almost one-tenth of the premiums written come from abroad. Quálitas is gradually building up similar businesses in Costa Rica (since 2011, 17% market share), El Salvador (2008, 7% share), Peru (2019, 7% share), and, more recently, Colombia. Foreign subsidiaries generally take around five years to reach profitability. El Salvador and Costa Rica already are profitable, Peru is expected to be so in 2025, and Colombia is just getting off the ground. In addition, Quálitas has an interesting business in the south of the United States, where it mainly insures cross-border freight (since 2011, with a 45% market share), directly benefiting from the growing trade between Mexico and the United States. Apart from Quálitas, there are only two other insurers in this inconspicuous but interesting corner of the market. In its foreign expansion, Quálitas prefers organic growth and to calmly and methodically grow its market share.

In Mexico, part of Quálitas's business has taken the form of vertical expansion. This part of the company is growing rapidly. Revenues grew from 39 million pesos in 2019 to 666 million pesos in 2023. The two main subsidiaries are Flekk, which is engaged in the purchase, sale, and service of automotive replacement parts and glass repair, and Autos y Salvamentos, which works in the management of crashed and mostly heavily damaged cars. In 2021, Quálitas established a completely new business line. Its subsidiary QSalud will sell health insurance. Between auto insurance and health insurance, I can imagine many synergies in sales, risk management, investments, and operations, and it could one day be a large and profitable business. The combination of low health insurance penetration in Mexico and good demographics holds great long-term business potential. Again, while taking a calm and methodical management approach, this cannot be expected to happen quickly. For the time being, this segment is so small that it does not require a separate line item in the financial statements.

Looking to the future, we expect Quálitas to produce an ROE of around 25% per annum, to maintain a high dividend payout ratio, and to grow its written premiums at a rate approaching 10% per annum over the long term. Quálitas should maintain the largest market share in Mexico and its foreign expansion should push its share of premiums written above 10% percent of the whole. We believe this to be an exceptional company in terms of quality, market position, management, and growth potential, outperforming even most comparable companies in developed markets. The opportunity to buy its stock today at approximately 10 times earnings strikes us as an attractive proposition. If an investor doesn't buy the stock too dearly to begin with, then reinvesting the dividends (minus their tax) should bring its long-term yield close to the long-term average ROE. This is as true for insurance companies as it is for banks. There are a great many hidden treasures in emerging markets. Finding them is more difficult than in developed markets, and there are various landmines to step around along the way. I would not base our investment portfolio predominantly on emerging market equities. That would be too risky. In individual cases, however, it makes a lot of sense to supplement the portfolio with carefully selected emerging market diamonds. A large proportion of these diamonds are not included in any key equity indices and so passively invested money largely avoids them. This is a beautiful playing field that active investors have almost entirely to themselves.

Chapter 16

Teekay Energy Partners

Seeking Treasure in the Pockets of Passive Investors

Like Ariadne's thread guiding Theseus through the Minotaur's labyrinth, there has been a strand running through this book and its individual chapters intended to lead the reader to an understanding of how the dominance of passive investing has changed the functioning and nature of the market while offering enormous benefits to active investors. Individual investment examples then show where and how value can be found in equities. Exchange-traded funds (ETFs) are the main instruments used by passive investors. ETFs do not, however, represent the majority of passively invested money. There are many additional ways to invest passively, but for ordinary passive investors, ETFs are the most common instrument of choice. An ETF is a basket of securities that can be traded on an exchange through brokerage firms. ETFs are offered for virtually every possible asset class, ranging from traditional investments to such so-called alternative assets as commodities or currencies. In addition, innovative ETF structures allow investors to sell markets short, trade with leverage, and avoid short-term capital gains taxes. Around 10,000 different ETFs are traded on exchanges today. I would place their actual start in 1993, when an S&P 500 index ETF began trading on the NYSE with the ticker SPY and the slang nickname "Spider." ETFs differ from regular investment funds in several ways. The main differences are that they are exchange traded, are traded throughout the full trading day, and have a large secondary market. ETFs are regarded to be among the most important innovations in the financial markets. What also can be seen in the case of ETFs, however, is how a good idea taken too far can bring large and previously unrecognized risks. For ETFs, these risks stem primarily from their enormous momentum and also from the very nature of their operation. Enough has been written about the risks and impact of the dominance of passive investing. In this chapter, I want to focus on the risk stemming from the difference between the perceived liquidity of some ETFs and the actual liquidity of their underlying assets.

It shouldn't be too surprising that ETFs have gained much popularity among investors. They allow easy access to various markets, sectors, and asset classes and have low costs. They can be low cost because there is no money management involved and no analytical work is required. They are de facto products aimed at accumulating assets and moving them automatically to wherever the composition of the index or basket they replicate dictates. ETFs are successful in accumulating assets, and it is in their huge overall size that the risk lies.

ETFs are quite specific in their structure and mechanism of operation. Each ETF has its own issuer. The issuer of an ETF is a management company that creates and markets the ETF. Some management companies specialize directly in ETFs, while other issuers may have broader activities. For example, they may be banks or larger investment companies. The largest issuers are BlackRock, Vanguard, State Street, Invesco, and Charles Schwab. In Europe, Amundi is a big player. The issuer determines the focus of the ETF, collects the management fees, and also selects other entities involved in running the ETF. The most important is the so-called "authorized participant" (AP). Typically, these are large investment banks such as Bank of America, JPMorgan Chase,

Goldman Sachs, and Morgan Stanley. Their role in the operation of ETFs is key. The attractiveness of ETFs is based on the fact that their price replicates the value of the assets that the ETF holds. The AP's main role is to create and redeem ETF shares. If an ordinary investor owns shares in an ETF, they can trade them on an exchange. If there exists an excess supply or excess demand on the exchange, however, the price of an ETF's shares would deviate from the value of the underlying assets in search of their equilibrium market price. In this situation, APs can step into the market and rebalance the market by issuing new shares in the event of an overhang of demand or buying back shares in the event of an overhang of supply. This ensures that, in the normal functioning of the market, the price of an ETF's shares closely follows the value of the underlying basket of assets held by that ETF. The AP is motivated to do this by arbitrage profits. If a situation arises in which the prices of the ETF's underlying assets are lower than the price of the ETF's shares in the market, the AP may purchase a representative basket of these assets in the market, deliver them to the ETF, and demand newly issued ETF shares in exchange. If the market prices of the ETF's underlying assets are higher than the ETF's share price, the AP may use arbitrage in the opposite direction.

This mechanism works well most of the time and for most ETFs. A stumbling block, however, is that APs are under no obligation to perform this activity and scarcely can be expected to be willing to commit themselves to it. The reason is simple. The arbitrage described is not always possible. In some wild stock market periods, it is limited by the high price volatility and low liquidity of the underlying assets. In this situation, the price of the ETF may become detached from the value of the underlying assets.

The larger the ETFs as a whole and individually, the more AP capacity they require to potentially maintain the balance between the ETF price and the underlying asset prices. We can more or less only speculate as to what are the capacity and willingness of APs to perform this function, as well as about their approach to limiting risk by lowering risk limits in the face of dramatic market events. In essence, then, in turbulent times, we can expect with a not inconsiderable probability that a large disconnect may indeed occur between ETF prices and the prices of the underlying assets. ETFs may trade at a large price discount, and their trading may even be suspended.

The Coronavirus Poured Sand into the ETF Gears

March 2020 demonstrated that this is not just an academic debate. Some ETFs, and especially those representing bonds, came under a lot of selling pressure. Some parts of the bond market essentially froze up. Many bonds were barely traded, liquidity evaporated, ETFs could not trade them, and their NAV calculations were based on unrealistic prices. APs had no ability in this situation to arbitrage to push ETF prices and NAVs to equilibrium levels, and doing so was probably about the last thing on their minds in those turbulent days. The cost from the lack of liquidity translated into huge discounts for some bond ETFs. The discounts averaged more than 5% across all bond ETFs, as much as 13% for high investment grade bond ETFs and up to 27% for low investment grade bond ETFs (Deghi et al., 2022). A gradual correction occurred only when the U.S. Federal Reserve announced that it would be buying also bond ETFs, but by that time great damage had already been done.

We had already suspected that such a situation might arise. When this did occur, it was evident in the prices of some stocks, bonds, and preferred shares that, in addition to the general panic in the markets, their declines were due to significant disruption in the functioning of the markets. The role of ETFs in this was obvious. In a letter to shareholders published in early April 2020, in the midst of a major market decline, we wrote about buying four new stocks. We described one of them as follows:

---

the fourth is a special opportunity where we expect a shorter holding period. We have been pointing out for some time already that the fact most money is managed by passive or covertly passive funds will mean that as soon as investors start to withdraw money from these funds, the funds will have difficulties to find enough buyers. This is exactly what happened in March and especially ETFs whose promised liquidity is higher than is the liquidity of the assets they hold had problems with it. They had no choice other than to sell out their positions at nearly any price. This created attractive opportunities, and we took advantage of one of these. It provides a beautiful example of how easily wealth can shift from passive to active investors. If the proportion of passively invested money will continue to grow, these opportunities will appear with ever increasing frequency.

We did not mention which stock it was at that time, because the attractive opportunity to purchase was still there, and we did not want to reveal our know-how, from which our investors pay to benefit and not to be broadcast to the whole world. Now we can say that it was a series B of Teekay Energy Partners (TGP) preferred shares. These are cumulative preferred shares with nominal value of $25 and dividend of $2.125, which means a dividend yield of 8.5% when the price is $25. TGP was a company operating a large fleet of liquefied natural gas tankers and its business was based on long-term contracts as long as 25 years. It was a very stable and predictable business.

A well-known rule says that some of the best investments originate in transactions where on one side there is somebody who is compelled to buy or sell, against their will, and regardless of price and liquidity. This is not just some academic fairy tale. Such opportunities really do arise, and our purchases of TGP-B shares fall into that category. Under normal circumstances, TGP-B shares traded at the level of their nominal value or even above. The dividend yield at these prices was very attractive and, in view of TGP's strong fundamentals, also relatively safe. The shares were not very liquid, having average daily traded volume of around 25,000 shares. The total number of shares outstanding was 6,800,000. Their low liquidity was partially given by the fact that a non-negligible portion of the shares were held by various index funds and ETFs. This also had something to do with an investment opportunity in the shares that opened up in March 2020.

When most of the large economies were locked down and markets started to fall, a number of ETFs faced cash withdrawals. By their very nature, ETFs hold almost no cash. When investors withdraw money, therefore, the ETFs have to sell assets in order to obtain cash to redeem (i.e., buy back) their own shares and pay off the departing investors. There is nothing unusual about this. It is a mechanism common to essentially all open funds, including ETFs. The ETFs themselves ensure daily and practically unlimited liquidity to their investors. A problem arises, however, when there occur too many withdrawals in comparison to the liquidity of those assets held by an ETF, because ETFs' underlying portfolios are often much less liquid. An ETF focused on preferred shares had a big liquidity problem in the spring of 2020. If a fund held, for instance, even just 500,000 TGP-B shares and had to sell them quickly, and if the average daily liquidity in the market for those shares was normally just 25,000, then this relatively low liquidity would represent a substantial limitation.

If there is a reduction in the number of ETF shares outstanding, ETFs do not have the luxury of waiting to sell. At the end of the day, they must have the cash to pay out to those investors who are leaving. That means they must sell at practically any prices, whether they like it or not. So, they sell under pressure, against their will, and regardless of price. Sometimes they even have to sell whatever assets the markets will absorb at all, and the composition of their portfolios can start to look quite different from the index or asset basket they are supposed to replicate. If you look at the course of trades in TGP-B stock during the spring of 2020, you get a nice picture of the situation's urgency. The stock was still trading above its $25 par value in mid-February. Then the ETFs' forced sell-offs hit and the price began to plummet. The whole process culminated on March 18, during which day the price temporarily fell below $12 (see Figure 16.1).

At the price of $12, the dividend yield per share was 17.7%. We knew TGP quite well, and considering the long duration and type of their

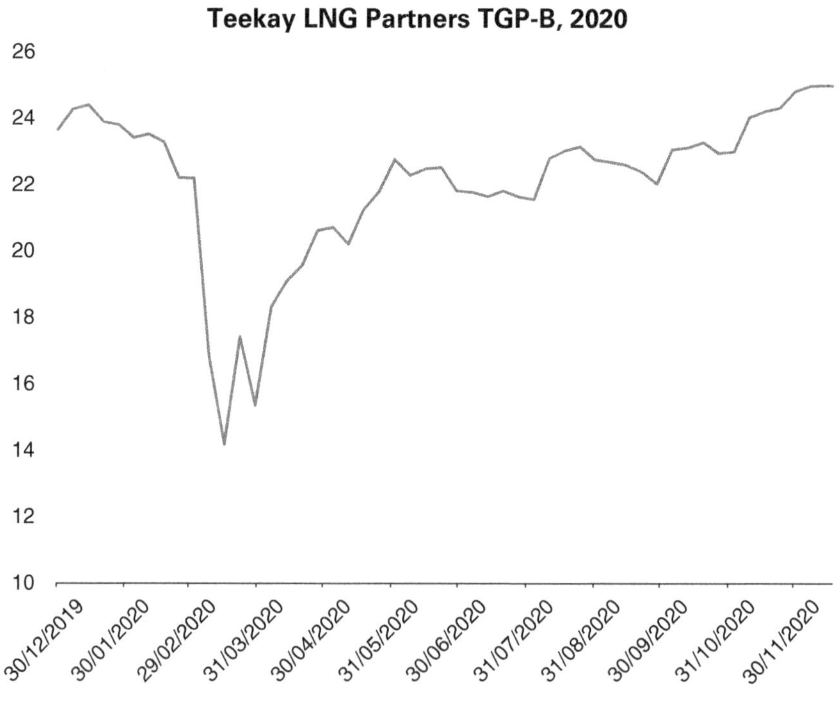

Figure 16.1   TGP preference share price (in USD) during 2020.
Source: Vltava Fund.

contracts, we were nearly certain that they would not be much affected by recession in 2020. (In the end, this proved to be a correct assumption because 2020 was a record year for TGP in all respects.) We were watching the price slump in real time, and we almost did not want to believe that somebody would be willing to sell us these shares for such low prices. In reality, however, and perhaps unfortunately, most of the final shareholders of those funds that were dumping the TGP-B shares into the market had no clue what was happening to their money. We viewed buying those shares as our only possible response. We assumed that the forced sell-offs would end sooner or later, the market would return to normal, and sooner or later the price of TGP's preference shares would go back to its usual level around $25. In addition to all this, there were big quarterly dividends coming and the price of money had fallen nearly to zero. This is exactly what happened. See Figure 16.2 shows that a similar but smaller such episode occurred in these shares at the end of 2018. We expect that similar situations will continue to appear in an ever-expanding spectrum of securities. The overwhelming dominance of passive investing causes the discrepancy between the

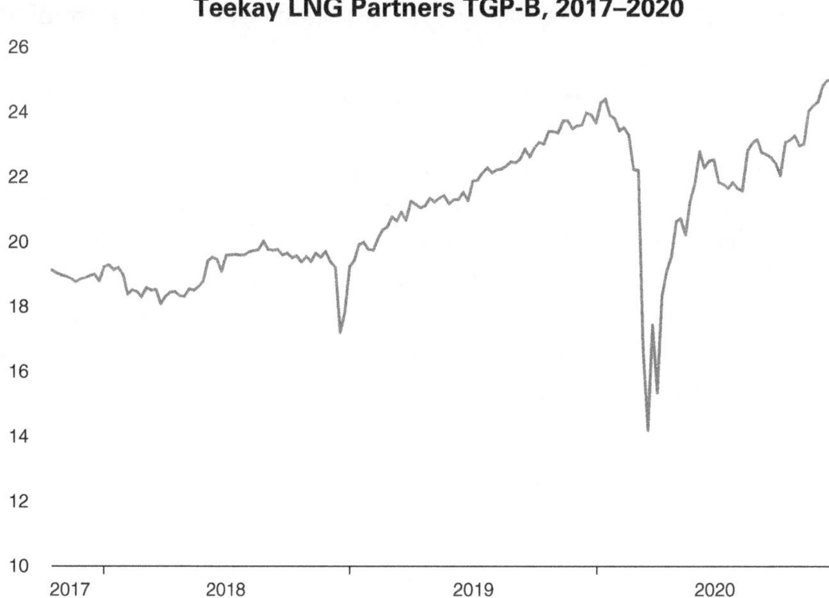

Figure 16.2 TGP preference share price in the period 2017–2020.
Source: Vltava Fund.

liquidity of ETFs themselves and that of their underlying assets to be increasing, and gradually this is affecting a larger part of the market. When money flows into these passive funds, they must buy – automatically and regardless of prices – as prescribed by their benchmarks. When money flows out, they must sell – again, automatically and regardless of prices.

Some readers may argue that almost all stocks fell significantly in the spring of 2020 and so in that respect TGP stock is no exception. This is true, but the TGP share, because of its preferential dividend, is more like a bond than a stock. A rational active investor would likely be on the buying side for these relatively safe preferred shares at a net interest yield in excess of 17%. By all indications, this was the case. An ETF was most certainly on the selling side. Its forced selling in a falling market with almost no liquidity resulted in significant losses for passive investors. There was literally a transfer of money from the pockets of passive investors into the pockets of active investors. Once the market stabilized and money started flowing into the ETFs again, these large passive investors were likely to start buying TGP's preferred shares again. But that wasn't until their price had doubled. The greater the dominance of passively invested money in the markets, the greater the likelihood that similar situations will occur again and again. Investors should keep this in mind when constructing their portfolios.

Of all the stocks that have been the focus of previous chapters, TGP's stock is the only one that is no longer in the Vltava Fund portfolio. In late 2021 and early 2022, the company was acquired by Stonepeak and TGP's common stock was taken off the market. We therefore sold our preferred shares at that time. Their price was back to par and, together with the large dividends paid, it had been a very profitable investment. I have included TGP into this book because its preferred shares provide a simple and illustrative example of how the prevalence of passively invested money can affect stock prices in actual practice.

Chapter 17

CVS and Microsoft

Two Examples of Different Investment Mistakes

I view investing as a matter of probabilities. Investing is not a natural science, and it has no laws – only certain patterns or regularities. In investing there is no objective truth, no objectively correct way, and no objectively correct value of a company. There exists always an element of uncertainty and an element of subjectivity. In our investment process, we try by its individual steps to tilt the probability of a good outcome in our favor. In the first step, we take care to avoid investing in something we don't understand. There are a quite a lot of things we don't understand, and it's important to be able to admit that. If I had to name one thing that causes investors to lose the most money, it's when they go into things they don't understand. If we can avoid these investments, the likelihood of a good outcome increases.

In the second step, we strive to make sure that a company has some sustainable competitive advantage. This can spring from a number of things, and it is important because, in long-term investing, we are interested in making sure that in 10 years' time the company not only still exists but also prospers. In the third step, we look for management to run the company for the benefit of shareholders and to allocate capital efficiently. We are interested in companies where there is significant long-term value creation. Companies that do not satisfy these conditions fall through our screen, and we don't spend more time on them. You could say that we see investing as a process of negative selection. Only in the cases of those companies satisfying the first three selection criteria do we try to estimate their intrinsic value. The result is a list of companies whose businesses and managements we like and that we understand, or at least we think we do. For each of these, we have an idea as to the price at which we would be willing to buy the shares. Most of the time, the majority of them are too expensive for our liking, and investing in them would be too risky for us. (Price is always an important element of risk.) So, we wait patiently for the time when the ratio between the share price and its value is favorable, and only then can we consider to include the stock into our portfolio. This entire process is repeating continuously. At the beginning of the process, there are several hundred companies that we monitor and analyze. At the end of the process is a portfolio with 20–25 different stocks.

While we believe that our investment process is well thought out and cautious, it is inevitable that from time to time we will make an investment that we must later regard as having been a mistake. If we look at our last 100 investments, which would mean going back as many as 15 years, it turns out that approximately 90% of our investments are profitable, and as many as 1 in 10 end in losses. There is no equating, however, the matter of whether an investment was profitable or loss-making and whether it was or was not a mistake.

If an investor buys a stock and its price goes up, one cannot automatically conclude that the right decision was taken. Likewise, just because an investor buys a stock and its price goes down does not automatically mean that an incorrect decision was taken. A bad outcome does not always reflect a bad decision. Markets and businesses are affected by many unpredictable factors, so good investment decisions can have negative results and vice versa. If the analysis of a business or investment was well thought through and based upon fundamentals, then a negative short-term outcome may not be a mistake. There is a fundamental difference between a bad outcome and a bad decision. The great investment legends from whom we can learn judge their own mistakes based primarily on the process that led to their decisions and not just on the outcomes. Important are the rules that investors have established for themselves, the ability to analyze a company's fundamentals, and an ability to correctly gauge the risks and values. They will admit a mistake if it turns out they underestimated key factors, changed their decision-making process based on emotions, or misunderstood the broader market context. In investing, it's good to view mistakes as a necessary part of an investor's development and try to learn from them. The key is to avoid repeating the same mistakes and to implement measures that will contribute to better decisions in the future. We ourselves have made plenty of investment mistakes in the past 20 years, and undoubtedly it will be no different in the future. In this chapter, I want to describe two of them.

CVS: A Stock We Never Should Have Bought

CVS Health Corporation is an American healthcare and pharmaceutical services company. Its business is to provide a wide range of healthcare and pharmaceutical services through its various divisions and offerings. CVS Health's key business areas include pharmacy services, pharmacy benefits management, medical clinics, and health insurance services, as well as home health and long-term care. Through its various divisions, CVS Health covers nearly all aspects of healthcare – from drug provision to insurance administration and patient care.

CVS used to be a popular stock in the markets. The share price growth, along with investor optimism, peaked sometime in mid-2015. After that, investor enthusiasm gradually began to wane, and criticism of management's asset allocation started to emerge. This dissatisfaction intensified, particularly in late 2017, when CVS announced the acquisition of health insurer Aetna for $69 billion. This price was absolutely exorbitant, and the acquisition also saddled CVS with a large debt burden for many years to come. The share price reacted with another significant drop. The stock came onto our radar in 2020, when it was cheap. CVS's business looked solid to us and was generating high free cash flow. Our positive view of the company was reinforced when CEO Larry Merlo announced his departure that year. He was the person behind the acquisition of Aetna, and the new CEO, Karen Lynch, who was formerly CEO of Aetna, announced that her main goals would include reducing debt and returning excess cash to shareholders. The regrettable acquisition of Aetna was not her doing, and she had a good reputation as Aetna's CEO. We succumbed to the belief that overpriced acquisitions were a thing of the past and that new management would allocate the company's capital more efficiently. That was our mistake. For a while, it looked like management was on the right track and the share price was rising. But then management reverted to the earlier acquisition practices. CVS announced two more large acquisitions in 2022 and 2023. These were Signify Health and Oak Street Health. The prices of both acquisitions made no sense to us at all. We realized that relying on management to behave rationally in terms of capital allocation was not enough, particularly in a company where this had not been the case previously. So, we started gradually to reduce our position in CVS, and now it is no longer in the portfolio. Had we reacted faster, we could have made more money on it. Our gain or loss came to around zero when dividends received were taken into account, so this investment had almost no impact on the overall return of the fund, but the money could have been much better invested during this time. In any case, we consider CVS to be our biggest buying mistake of recent years. In the hands of more capable management and with a rational allocation of capital, CVS stock could be at three times its price today. In this case, we underestimated the negative impact of the human factor on the value of the company. This was and remains an important lesson for the future.

We knew that acquisitions, and especially large acquisitions, often have negative impact on the value of companies. I have written about this at several places in previous chapters. We also knew that CVS had its own history of overpriced acquisitions, which we viewed critically from a shareholder perspective. We understood as well from our experience that company culture is often deeply rooted throughout an organizational structure and that it can be difficult to change. A change of CEO, moreover, if that person comes from within the company, is usually not enough to alter such behavior. Yet, for some reason, we put aside these objections and invested in CVS stock. Only because part of our investment process emphasizes low price did we not end up with an absolute loss of invested capital. Otherwise, however, we violated several points within our own investment process and therefore unequivocally regard this investment to have been a mistake. The lesson we take away from it is that our investment discipline needs to be stronger. That is the general conclusion.

Specific to this instance, we seem to have given preference to the "case rate" arguments over the "base rate" arguments.

In investing, the concepts of base rate and case rate are used in decision-making and risk assessment. *Base rate* refers to the general or historical probability that a particular event or outcome will occur within a broad sample or population. It can be described as a "background" rate that shows how often something happens on average while not taking into account the specific details of individual cases. Investors use baseline measures to make decisions based on broad patterns, such as the average returns of an asset class (stocks, bonds, etc.) over time. It can also be expedient to rely on a base measure to estimate profit margins or in reckoning long-term revenue growth rates and earnings per share. Historical averages and benchmarks help in setting expectations for the future. Knowing the base rate helps investors avoid overestimating specific information (such as concerning recent events) and take into account broader historical averages. It promotes a more objective and statistical approach to investing.

In contrast, a *case rate* measure refers to the probability or expectation of a particular event or outcome's occurrence in the context of a specific, individual case or situation. It is based on the distinctive characteristics and context of a given case and not on the general population. Investors then focus on a certain investment (a company, asset, or strategy) while analyzing the aspects of that case, such as the financial health of the company, quality of management, growth potential, and so forth. Case-by-case thinking emphasizes the distinctive details of a given situation rather than historical averages. An investor researching a particular company may evaluate its unique strengths (e.g., a new, breakthrough product) and conclude that it has a much higher probability of success than would be suggested by a base case measure for the industry.

Base case measures are associated with large groups or historical averages. Case rate refers to individual, specific cases or opportunities. Base rate focuses on long-term, broad patterns and probabilities. The case measure focuses on the specific details and context of an individual investment. Base rate thinking is more conservative and more consistent with historical trends. Case rate thinking can be riskier because it depends upon the uniqueness of the individual case, although it can lead to greater rewards if the estimations are correct. We strive to combine the two approaches. We start by trying to understand the base measure (i.e., historical market performance or industry trends) and then look at the specific case to see if it differs significantly from the average and, if so, why. In some cases, we lean toward the weight of the base measure; in others, we incline toward the weight of the case measure. In most instances, only time will tell which measure will prevail.

We also had considered base rate versus case rate in the matter of CVS and the impact of acquisitions on the value of the company. We knew that the base rate case spoke strongly against this investment. Acquisitions, and especially large acquisitions, more often reduce the value of a company rather than increase it. From a case rate perspective, meanwhile, history has not been positive for CVS either. The company had made a large and over-priced acquisition of Aetna, and there was nothing to justify the view that a substantial positive case rate outweighed the negative base rate. Both were flashing negative signals. Still, we were tempted by the apparent cheapness of the stock and the hopeful statements from the new CEO regarding future capital allocation. Essentially, we based our investment on the belief that things would get better. That is not enough of an argument to invest, and therefore we consider buying CVS stock to have been a mistake.

Microsoft: A Share We Should Never Have Sold

We regret the mistake we made when investing in Microsoft shares more than any other, even though it was a profitable investment. Microsoft is a universally well-known company and is one of the most popular stocks on the market today, but this was not always the case. We bought its shares in the second half of 2010. The price then was between \$20 and \$25, representing about 10 times earnings. From today's perspective, with Microsoft stock trading at a P/E of 36×, that seems incredible. Back then, the market simply didn't like Microsoft. Its share price was still a hair lower than it had been in 1999, and the prevailing view among investors was that it was a company that had nothing left to say and was gradually heading for the sidelines.

Our view was different. Our analysis led us to conclude that this was a strong and promising company, one that could adapt to changes in its industry. We found the share price to be low and almost irresistible. I remember well that when we added Microsoft to the Vltava Fund portfolio, we quite often had to defend this move to our shareholders because they, too, saw it as a step backward, as a company that had no future.

It took a while for the stock's price to start going up, but once it did, then everyone was happy. When we first bought the stock, Microsoft's earnings per share were $2.10. In the fiscal year ending June 2024, it was $11.80. That is an earnings gain of 4.6 times. Meanwhile, the stock price had climbed from an initial $22 to its current $430. That's almost 20 times. Along the way, there has been a complete change in most investors' view of Microsoft. Today, it is no longer considered a second-tier company. Today, Microsoft is a member of that revered group of companies known as the Magnificent 7. Perhaps it could be said that it has gone from being an unfairly underappreciated company to one the expectations for which are so optimistic that it will be quite difficult to live up to them.

Somewhere in the middle of this process, we sold the stock. In retrospect, it was too soon. I don't think we would have held onto the shares until today. Their market valuation is too high for that, but we could have held them a lot longer. Inasmuch as Microsoft was one of the largest positions in our portfolio, the amount of money we left on the table, so to speak, saddens me still to this day. I would describe our mistake as one of "anchoring." This is a typical psychological error in thinking. I like it best when we can buy established, profitable, and growing companies at five times earnings. Sometimes we are able to do it. Buying at 10 times earnings for a company like Microsoft can also be a nice moneymaker. The initial P/E of 10× then created an anchor in our minds to which we tied our assessment of the stock's attractiveness. When Microsoft's valuation began to rise along with its earnings, and its P/E rose to 12×, then to 15×, then to 17×, and even higher, one of the measurement gauges for us was the market valuation at which we had bought the stock. Because our purchase was made cheaply, the stock relatively soon began to look expensive. Yet the buying price and valuation at purchase should be irrelevant to an investor's subsequent decision-making, unless perhaps there were some tax implications. In short, not only in retrospect, but also taking into account the information we had available to us at the time of the sale, we were hasty in selling. We feel this to have been a painful mistake, even though the investment in Microsoft shares was profitable for us.

The lesson we take from this experience is that if we have a stock in our portfolio for a company that is doing well, and one that we know well, we are now willing to be more generous on valuation and to let the positive trend run longer. This approach cannot be taken automatically, but, if supported by careful analysis, it can sometimes be better to let a positive investment trend ride longer for several reasons. Together, these justifications can create a multiplier effect. A positive trend in the performance of the company itself does not just mean an increase in its profitability. This usually attracts the attention of other investors, too, and this is reflected in the stock's market valuation. As time passes and the share price grows, the advantage of compound interest becomes more and more apparent. Fewer transactions also mean lower transaction costs. Of course, the benefits are offset by the risk that it can be difficult to predict exactly when the trend will end. Nor is it easy to judge when it is beginning. Only with hindsight can a convincing judgment be made about the emergence of a trend, and at that point the trend may already have run its course. The majority of investment theories and most considerations by investors themselves revolve around the selection of individual investments. Much less attention is given to considerations of when to sell a stock, but the decision to sell is at least as important. The lessons learned from the Microsoft case have led us to pay more attention than we had previously to the question of when to sell.

The views having the most value in investing are those of a minority that turn out to be correct. They are the ones who have the most to gain. A correct view that is shared by the majority of investors, however, is not nearly so valuable. In fact, the majority view tends to be fully reflected in share prices. Our view of Microsoft and its stock was very much in the minority 14 years ago, and quite quickly it proved to be correct, but, unfortunately, we were unable to exploit its full potential. I consider our biggest mistakes to be the investments we sold too early. Microsoft is the flagship in that fleet.

Investing in equities is a process fraught with uncertainty and challenges, and making mistakes is an inevitable part of the process. Markets are dynamic and are influenced by a myriad of factors that an investor cannot fully control. Moreover, even the best analysis cannot predict future developments with absolute certainty. Sometimes I would even say that markets exist to remind investors that they are fallible. The key point is how an investor deals with mistakes. Rather than to be seen as failures, they should be taken as opportunities to learn and improve. It is indeed the errors that can teach investors the most important lessons. Each bad investment can reveal weaknesses in approach, strategy, or analysis, and ultimately this helps in future decisions. Making mistakes is a natural part of investing, but the right approach to these missteps can make an investor stronger. Instead of striving for perfection, the emphasis should be on continuous improvement and learning. Success in investing comes not from never making a mistake but from responding constructively to one's mistakes. It is quite probable that time will show me to be wrong on some points even in my analysis of some companies that are the subjects of all the preceding chapters. It would be irrational to expect that this would not be the case. But that is no argument for giving up the search for hidden investment treasures. Indeed, I think, quite the contrary.

Chapter 18

Berkshire Park

Years ago, my wife and I bought a piece of land that I call "Berkshire Park" (what else would I call it, right?). Her domain is flowers and shrubs, mine is trees. I love to plant trees, and I love to watch them grow. Watching trees grow is not a matter of days or weeks. It's a matter of many years. A person doesn't see any change from one day to the next, but when one looks back after a long time, it often is surprising just how much the trees have grown. I see a close analogy between this and investing in stocks. Picking individual investments for a portfolio is like planting trees. When we buy a stock for the Vltava Fund portfolio, it means for us, first and foremost, a stake in the business of one particular company. Share price movements are easy to see and often attract most of the attention, but, as long-term investors, we are primarily interested in how the company we own is doing in its business. It's a never-ending story that unfolds before our eyes, and one that we follow closely. As with trees, it is impossible to see any tangible growth or shift in individual companies from one day to the next. But, also like trees, when we look back over a period of years, the changes in the businesses of these companies and in their values tends to be enormous. If you examine what the companies I've described in previous chapters looked like 5, 10, or 15 years ago and compare them to where they are today, the changes in size and value are huge. Some of them are further along today by an order of magnitude or even two.

To continue the tree planting analogy, of all the trees I've ever planted, not every one of them has taken. That was to be expected. Some died for various reasons. But if all those that are still alive and growing could be moved to one place, it would be a big and beautiful forest. If a person wants to have a forest, then they must choose well what to plant in it, must take care of that forest, but, above all, must plant the trees to begin with. It's the same with stocks. By no means have all those I have ever bought – either together with my colleagues in our fund or privately before it was set up – taken off. Sometimes it was our fault; sometimes it was circumstances beyond our control. What has taken hold, however, now constitutes a great stock forest. As with real trees, stock trees need to be well selected and carefully looked after – but above all they need to be planted. Otherwise, there's nothing to grow.

In this book, I have tried to point out that the conditions for selecting individual stock trees today are quite ideal. Certainly, they are the best I've seen in my 31 years of investment experience. Investment theory says that the investor's job is to construct an investment portfolio that has the ideal combination of return and risk. This is no trivial task. Estimating returns on individual investments is not easy, and investment risk is often either misunderstood or underappreciated. Nevertheless, the state and development of the stock markets make this task easier than it used to be. This is due to its declining level of efficiency. With a broader view to the good functioning of an economy, it would be desirable for stock markets to be as efficient as possible. Indeed, the primary reason for the existence of stock markets is to enable individual firms to raise capital for their businesses and to allow capital to be directed to its best use. The relative prices of individual shares and their overall level are the main incentives for capital deployment.

I recall from five years ago, while reading the annual report of the Canadian company Constellation Software, I had come across an interesting sentence. In his introductory letter to shareholders, Mark Leonard (2018), the company's founder and chief executive, had written that "(index investors) buy our stock because we are part of whatever index they are emulating. Their actions are formulaic. Despite the fact that they may be long-term

holders, it is difficult to find someone to speak with at these indexing institutions and even if we do, they rarely know much about our company."

This sentence captures well what disturbs me about index investing.
Index investing makes the market even more inefficient by suppressing its
price-discovery function and ultimately constraining the performance of
the economy as a whole. The prevalence of passive investing is not the
only reason for the declining efficiency of stock markets. Another cause is
the existence of social networks and developments in technology. Never
before has so much data and information been so easily and cheaply
accessible to such a broad population as it is today. At the same time, never
before has it been so easy and inexpensive as it is today to trade anytime,
anywhere at the snap of a finger. It would seem that the conditions for
efficient resource allocation are ideal. Yet, I think they are leading to a
reduction in the efficiency of stock markets. Investing is not about having
as much information as possible and being able to use it as quickly as possible. Investing is all about being able to make the proper judgments. To
do that, paradoxically, you only need a fraction of all the data available to
an investor today. The ready availability of enormous amounts of data and
information and the possibility to react to this almost instantaneously
without any constraints leads to a false sense of control and to impulsive
behavior. Social networks then tend to push investors to succumb more
easily to the narratives of the moment and to the herd mentality. There is
a pithy quote on this subject from Warren Buffett and Berkshire Hathaway's
2023 annual report: "markets now exhibit far more casino-like behavior
than they did when I was young. The casino now resides in many homes
and daily tempts the occupants."

Wise investors know they cannot change the state of the markets. An
active investor might not even want to change it. They realize that they
are playing their cards very well and that there are various ways of working the situation to their advantage. According to data from S&P Global,
which compiles the S&P 500 index, as of the end of September 2024, the
reported earnings per share of the companies in the index over the past
12 months were $202. The index itself closed September at a value of
5,762. That translates to a P/E of 28.5×. (Note: investors often prefer to
use operating earnings instead of reported earnings. That mainly is because
operating earnings are usually higher and so make the market appear less
expensive. The P/E measured in this way was 25.3× as of the end of
September 2024. The 20-year average of this multiple is 18.9×.) That is a

very high number, compared both to its historical values and to likely or even possible earnings growth. The index's earnings per share as of September 2014 had been $105. So, over the course of years, earnings have grown by 92%. That's about 6.8% a year. In September 2004, the index's EPS was $57. The growth was therefore 254% over 20 years (6.6% per year). Over the long term, the index has been fairly consistent in growing earnings at just under 7% per annum. The value of the index, however, has recently risen much faster. Since September 2014, the index has increased by 192%, and it has grown by 421% since September 2004. Its rise, therefore, has far outpaced that of earnings. If passive investors, who often buy the index today on the argument that it has delivered good returns in recent years, expect similar returns in the future, they are likely to be disappointed. Extrapolating recent returns into the future tends to be one of the costliest of investors' errors. It is not probable that the P/E of the index will continue to rise significantly and to hit such values as 30×, 35×, or even 40×. This is what would be required were the index to deliver returns to passive investors comparable to those of the past decade while maintaining the usual level of earnings growth in the companies making up the index. That could happen, of course, purely as a theoretical matter, but basing an investment on this wishful thinking is not rational. Would you invest in a stock with a P/E approaching 30× and whose long-term earnings are only growing at a rate of less than 7% per year? Hardly. In buying the index, however, that is exactly what passive investors are getting for their money. That the rate of growth in the profits of the U.S. companies included in the index as a whole will differ significantly from historical averages in the future is not very likely.

There are other arguments for caution when anticipating future returns from the S&P 500. The five largest companies in the index have a combined market capitalization of $13.6 trillion. They are Apple, Microsoft, Nvidia, Alphabet, and Amazon. The U.S. gross domestic product in 2023 was $27.3 billion. The Big Five, therefore, have a combined market capitalization equal to half of GDP. To paraphrase Nassim Taleb, I would say that this is not a situation that could be called "antifragile." If these five stocks are to continue in delivering high returns to investors, there must be yet another significant shift in this statistic. If the five largest companies were to deliver a return to investors of 10% p.a. over the next 10 years – and which some might even consider a disappointment compared to current expectations – their combined market capitalization would have to rise to \$35.3 trillion. Now, if GDP were to grow at 4% per year in nominal terms, which would be nice and would require the absence of major recessions, it would climb to \$40 trillion. Is it rational to expect that the five largest companies will have a combined capitalization equal to 87% of GDP? I wouldn't bet on it, and I wouldn't bet on a high index return either. That combination of expected return and risk seems to me highly unfavorable. One could hardly expect anything else in a situation where huge amounts of money from passive investors are making the indices and their largest constituents more and more expensive.

Risk

The fragility of the U.S. market is no reason for investors to shun stocks, but it is a reason to avoid passively investing in indices. For active investors, this may represent a golden age. They can completely ignore those parts of the market that passive investing makes unattractive and devote themselves to finding hidden investment treasures in places where the passive investor's eye cannot see. A portfolio that they can assemble from these investments may not only have a much higher expected return than do the major indices, but it also may have much lower risk. Risk is a concept and category that is often forgotten. When people talk about investing, the discussion most commonly turns to returns. They discuss the returns of individual stocks, indices, portfolios, over various past time intervals, and expected returns in the future. I have written about this before, but, interestingly, in all my 30+ years of practice, I have never been asked the question: "How much risk do you have in your portfolio?" It's as if no one cares about risk. Yet, returns and risk are two sides of the same coin. The two cannot be separated. And without an idea as to the level of risk, you cannot evaluate returns. This is understandable to a certain extent, because while return is well and objectively measurable and everybody can imagine what a return of, say, 50% means, risk is more problematic. There are three reasons in particular for that to be the case. First, there is no objective definition of risk. Second, risk is not precisely measurable. Third, this is in large measure a subjective category. What seems too risky to one person may seem just fine to another, and vice versa. One often hears the argument that to achieve higher returns one needs to take on more risk. This is in fact not the case, and I will try briefly to explain why.

So, what is investment risk? How can it be defined? Well, let's start with what risk definitely is not. Risk is not equal to volatility. Standard financial theory often defines risk as the price volatility for a given asset. The more volatile its price has been in the past, the more risk that is attributed to the asset. Unfortunately, this approach to risk is completely mistaken. The historical volatility of an asset's price tells you only one thing — how much the price has fluctuated. It tells you nothing about what the investment risk of the asset has been, what its future investment risk will be, or even what its future volatility will be. So why is risk often measured in this way? With just a modest dose of cynicism, I would say it is because volatility can be measured and, in doing so, elegant mathematics are used that most people do not understand, thereby giving the people who make such reckonings an aura of academic sophistication.

But when you look not at what academic theorists but rather investment legends like Warren Buffett, Charlie Munger, Benjamin Graham, Seth Klarman, Francois Rochon, Nick Sleep, and others have to say about understanding risk as volatility, you find yourself in a completely different mindset. That way of thinking regards ill-considered investments as the main source of risk, and it welcomes volatility as a source of opportunity.

I'll try to show the fundamental difference in this style of thinking by the following simplified example. Suppose your investment objective is to beat inflation over the long term. This is a perfectly realistic and reasonable goal in practice — to strive to increase the real value of your invested amounts. What will be the source of risk for you in this case? The risk will be something that will threaten or even prevent you from achieving this goal. If you base your investments on holding cash, you will achieve the lowest possible volatility. According to standard financial theory, your portfolio will therefore have minimal risk. In practice, however, this will ensure that you will never achieve your investment goal of real appreciation, because the real value of money declines over time. Cash therefore represents the greatest risk in terms of the probability of achieving your investment goal. As Warren Buffett says, stocks are more volatile than cash or bonds, but they are safer in the long run.

So, if we leave volatility to the theorists, how do we define risk in practice? Above all, we must abandon the idea that risk can be reduced to a number. In my view, risk is not measurable — certainly not ex ante but not even ex post. Physics knows a number of quantities that can be measured. These include length, trajectory, time, speed, mass, temperature, force, pressure, work, power, energy, and so forth. But risk cannot in any case be thought about in this way. Risk takes many forms, falls into numerous categories, and has unclear boundaries. Moreover, as I said, risk always bears an element of subjectivity. So how do we understand investment risk? We understand risk as a question of probabilities, and we try to tilt the probability of a good return in our direction by taking particular steps. We consider the following three elements of risk to be key: awareness as to the limits of our own abilities and skills, avoiding the risk of permanent loss, and emphasizing price.

To reiterate, if I had to name one thing that causes investors to lose the most money, it's when they get into things they don't understand. I would say this is true for all types of investments and for all investors regardless of their experience. We try to avoid this risk as much as possible by paying close attention to where are the boundaries of what we (probably) understand and what we (almost certainly) do not understand. We then concentrate our investments only in areas that lie within this imaginary circle of competence. Although we are gradually trying to expand our knowledge, we fully admit that there are many things still beyond our reach. Our investing is based on exploiting the differences between the price and value of individual stocks. It is quite challenging to estimate with a reasonable degree of applicability the value of a company whose business we do understand. It would be quite absurd to think that it is possible to do so for companies that we do not understand. Remaining within the boundaries of our circle of competence is the most important element of risk management in our investing.

The second pillar of our risk management is to avoid the risk of permanent loss of capital. Or, better said, to minimize its probability. A permanent loss of capital is a situation in which an investor loses part (or even all) of invested capital on a particular investment without being able to recover it. We don't need to go far to find examples of permanent loss of capital. In the spring of last year, there was a minor banking crisis in the United States during which several banks failed. Two of the best known of these were Silicon Valley Bank and First Republic Bank. Both banks went into receivership and investors lost all their money. This capital is therefore gone forever, with no possibility of recovering it.

Permanent loss of capital is not the same as volatility. Share prices fluctuate normally. A difference of 40% between the highest and lowest price of a given share during the year is not unusual. For the long-term investor, however, volatility is not a source of risk. The source of risk is the permanent loss of capital. How do we try to avoid it? We know from experience that the most common causes of permanent loss of capital tend to be poor quality businesses, high levels of debt, and poor management actions. It is often the case, too, that these three causes occur together. Therefore, even with regard to companies we understand, we try to focus our investments primarily on those that have high returns on capital and strong free cash flow (a sign of quality), have minimal, often no debt, and have management that allocates capital efficiently and does not make big mistakes such as overpriced acquisitions or investments with low rates of return. Looking back over the past 15 years, I can find several instances of retrospectively successful investments that we did not make because it would have required too much risk at the time of decision-making. Nevertheless, among the 100 or so investments we did make within that same period, there is not a single one that I could describe as resulting in a permanent loss of capital. We have set our risk limits quite low, and I think (altogether subjectively) that this is a good thing.

The final essential element of risk management is our emphasis on good price. It is quite obvious that the same stock will present a different level of risk at prices of $20, $200 or $2,000 (the same in any other currencies). Indeed, price is always a key element of risk. For each investment, we try to ensure that the price of the shares we buy is significantly below their value. Risk management here consists of three parts. First, we only try to estimate value for those companies where we can do so with an acceptable degree of confidence. We avoid stocks where this cannot be done, as this would be pure speculation. Second, we try to reach actual value estimates that are conservative and realistic. Third, the margin of safety between price and value really has to be quite wide. In practice, it is this last condition that often ensures to a large extent that even if we make a mistake in our judgment about the value of a company and its development, the investment can still be profitable.

The individual steps of our risk management approach are not measurable, some of them are even difficult to estimate, but all of them together are designed to eliminate the important risk elements that exist and thus over time tilt the probability of a good return in our favor. The result, or so we hope, is a portfolio that is far less risky than the overall market portfolio. We think we know quite a lot about the companies we invest in. By contrast, an investor who buys a broad market portfolio of hundreds or thousands of companies has to accept that he or she knows nothing about the vast majority of them. Our approach presents lower risk. The companies we own, taken as a whole, are of a higher quality than the market average. They have higher returns on equity and higher returns on capital. They have incomparably less debt than the market average. Some of them even have no debt at all. This makes them more resilient and less dependent on external financing. In our view, their management have the important ability to allocate capital efficiently in addition to the ability to manage the business itself. This is a rare but very important skill upon which we place great emphasis. It has a major impact on creating the long-term value of a company. A large part of our portfolio is made up of companies that are controlled either by their founders or by a key shareholder for whom these assets are personally absolutely critical. This makes it more likely that the interests and motivations of the company's management coincide with those of the shareholders, and much more so than is typical for an average company in the market. In our understanding of risk, it is possible to construct an attractive growth stock portfolio that will have an expected return that is better than the expected return of the index, while at the same time bearing much less risk than that of the overall market. Today's market conditions are ideal for this.

In the individual chapters, I have tried to show, using selected companies as examples, that an active investor has the ability to find value in individual stocks in a variety of ways and that the opportunities are indeed many – even many more than any one person can find. I could go on writing more chapters on other companies, either those that we also own at Vltava Fund or those that we know but do not currently own. Then, too, there must still be many attractive investment opportunities of which we are not yet aware and just waiting to be discovered. In writing this, however, I have limited myself to only those companies that are in our portfolio today, because I think that situations where investors put their money where their mouths are have more credibility. In addition, I have tried to ensure that for each of the companies I have chosen there is some investment theme that can be described and explained, has long-term validity, and is applicable to the analysis of other companies as well.

This book should not be seen as a set of investment tips and an incentive to invest in the companies described. If I may be allowed to give one piece of advice, never buy a stock just because someone else has it or because someone says it is a good investment. You can take that as inspiration or an idea of what to focus on, but before you put money into a stock, your own careful analysis must precede it. Then stick to your own opinion, whether it is the same or different. We own all the companies that are the subjects of each chapter, and we think we know exactly why.

It is likely that a large number of them will be in our portfolio for many years to come. But it is also likely, or I should say even certain, that some will not be there. There may be various reasons, and one of them may be that we are simply wrong in our analysis for some of the selected companies. It would not be the first time, and it would not be the last. Even today, among those of us involved in our fund, we are not all of the same opinion on all stocks. That's a good thing, and it would be strange were it otherwise. It is far more beneficial for an investor to confront views that are different when testing his own investment thesis than to seek out views that support his own.

A person also should be able and willing to change one's mind if circumstances change. My colleague at the fund, Jan Žák, told me that if I would write the book the way I did, it will be more difficult for us to change our minds about the stocks described. Publicly committing to certain investments will create a barrier to our freedom of thought. I believe this will not be the case. In our letters to shareholders, which we also publish quarterly on our website www.vltavafund.com, we always describe changes in our portfolio. You can sign up to receive them automatically and see for yourself how long individual stocks in this book last in our portfolio and which ones must step aside to make way for other investments. I'm curious about that myself, and I look forward to the hidden investment treasures we have yet to discover.

As I was thinking about how to end this book, I told myself that some metaphor would be appropriate here. But I'm not adept at writing these, so in the end, I thought I'd resort to a simple trick. One of my musical idols is Bob Dylan. Among other things, one of the things I admire about him is his way with words. He's a Nobel Prize winner for literature and a Pulitzer Prize winner. This is totally unprecedented for a musician, but completely deserved. I imagined how Dylan might write the last paragraph of this book. I'll always have the option of subscribing to it or disavowing it.

"Investing in stocks? That's like driving down the highway with the wind at your back and the sun over your head. The stock market, you know, it's always a-changin', it's a dance between heaven and earth, like the wind playin' in the leaves on the trees. Sometimes you're flyin' high, 'n' sometimes you're sinkin' down deep. It's all a risk, ain't it? But what's it matter if you know the journey's never gonna end? Sometimes it's intuition, other times it's all planned out. But it's like in music, it's about timing – knowing when to hold on and when to let go. You can win, you can lose, but the main thing is to keep on movin'. That's life, that's investing."

Bibliography

Bouchouev, I. (2023). *Virtual Barrels: Quantitative Trading in the Oil Market*. Springer Texts in Business and Economics.

Deghi, A., Gan, Z.K., Guérin, P., et al. (2022). Asset Price Fragility in Times of Stress: The Role of Open-end Investment Funds. In: *Global Financial Stability Report*. International Monetary Fund.

Flatt, B. (2024). *Letter to Shareholders, Q2 2024*. Brookfield Corporation.

Gladiš, D. (2021). *Akciové investice (Equity Investing)*. Grada Publishing.

Katz, R. (2024). *The Contest for Japan's Economic Future*. Oxford University Press.

Leonard, M. (2018). *2017 President's Letter*. Constellation Software.

Mauboussin, M. and Callahan, D. (2023). *Total Shareholder Return: Linking the Drivers of Total Returns to Fundamentals*. Morgan Stanley Investment Management.

McNally, R. (2019). *Crude Volatility: The History and the Future of Boom-Bust Oil Prices*. Columbia University Press.

Mead, A.J. (2021). *The Complete Financial History of Berkshire Hathaway: A Chronological Analysis of Warren Buffett and Charlie Munger's Conglomerate Masterpiece*. Petersfield, Hampshire: Harriman House.

Miller, C. (2022). *Chip War: The Fight for the World's Most Critical Technology*. Scribner.

OPEC. (2023). *2023 World Oil Outlook 2045*. Organization of the Petroleum Exporting Countries.

Schaede, U. (2020). *The Business Reinvention of Japan: How to Make Sense of the New Japan and Why it Matters*. Stanford University Press.

Semper Augustus Investment Group LLC. (2024). *Dirty Deeds Done Dirt Cheap, 2023 Letter to Clients*.

Smil, V. (2022). *How the World Really Works: A Scientist's Guide to Our Past, Present and Future*. Penguin Random House UK.

Udland, M. (2017). Jack Bogle envisions 'chaos, catastrophe' in markets if everyone were to index. *Yahoo! Finance* (6 May).

About the Author

Daniel Gladiš has been an active stock investor since the early 1990s. He continues today in managing the Vltava Fund, which he founded in 2004. *Hidden Investment Treasures* is his third book. His first two books, *Learn to Invest* (2004) and *Stock Investing* (2014), were published in Czech by Grada Publishing. Gladiš lives in Brno, Czech Republic, and spends his free time with his family, cross-country skiing, studying, and traveling.

Index

Page numbers followed by *f* and *t* refer to figures and tables, respectively.